PRAISE FOR

HEAVENLY HINDSIGHTS

"With over a decade in experience with energy work and my passion for Quantum Healing Hypnosis Technique and past-life regression, I highly recommend *Heavenly Hindsights* to anyone that is seeking healing in this life or another. Grief is inevitable, but it doesn't have to destroy us. We are capable of self-healing and highly capable of adjusting our surroundings with intent and personal power, and Linda proves this in her book. We are never separate from our loved ones or ourselves. *Heavenly Hindsights* is life changing and will bring healing, joy, and peace to your soul."

—**MELANIE AGUIRRE,** Starseed Solutions, Past-Life Regressionist

"Every bereaved parent has a unique journey to the quiet phase of grief. We don't forget; we always remember and find a way to live our lives. Linda not only shows the path she took for healing, she shows how this journey created a profound path of meaning for her. The healing ends and life begins anew. I applaud Linda for finding her path and sharing it with us."

—**RADHA STERN,** Author of *Griefprints: A Practical Guide for Supporting a Grieving Person,* Steering Committee Member: The Compassionate Friends

"In *Heavenly Hindsights*, Linda joins her voice with her son, Patrick, to create an understanding of the personal and spiritual meaning of what happened during his life and his death. Her courageous, authentic, and sincere journey of self-discovery has led her to profound life lessons and spiritual truths that she outlines in each chapter, along with references to sources she has found helpful. That she has found peace and meaning is a hopeful message for others also seeking to understand the death of a loved one, rise above the pain, and apply what is learned to continued healing and growth."

—REV. BARBARA MEYERS, Author of *Held: Showing Up For Each Other's Mental Health*; Mental Health Community Minister; Mission Peak Unitarian Universalist Congregation

"Linda Kolsky provides a compelling and comforting perspective of life, and our existence before and after life, as we conventionally think of it. Using personal experience, her own training, and a multitude of references, Ms. Kolsky guides us through her life and that of her son, both before and after (in the case of her son) their current incarnations; the organization of her material makes for gripping reading. The exposure she provides to this area of thought was engaging for me, a nonpracticing Catholic, and I drew much comfort from the idea that there is a plan for me and my loved ones, even if the elements of those plans aren't always carefree and without pain. This book imparts understanding and provides substance to the overused, under-explained statement, 'It's all part of God's plan.' The book goes into quite some depth in areas of spiritual thought that initially felt unfamiliar to me and, after several repeated readings, felt cohesive and tangible; much food for thought here. I look forward to reading *Heavenly Hindsights* several more times, to explore other references and to appreciate more fully the spiritual concepts that Ms. Kolsky has so compellingly explored."

—SUSAN COLEMAN, Realtor, Marin Home Properties

Heavenly Hindsights:
How One Mother Found Meaning in Life
After the Death of Her Child

by Linda Kolsky

ISBN 978-1-64663-570-2

Published by

 köehlerbooks™

3705 Shore Drive
Virginia Beach, VA 23455
800-435-4811
www.koehlerbooks.com

HEAVENLY HINDSIGHTS

How One Mother Found Meaning in Life After the Death of Her Child

LINDA KOLSKY

VIRGINIA BEACH
CAPE CHARLES

This book is dedicated to my husband, Alan, who has been the quiet but ever-present strength behind this work. This would not have happened without you! And to my daughter, Lauren, thank you for your enthusiasm and especially for inspiring me to look at life in a different way, filled with love and amazement.

Table of Contents

Introduction

LIFE IS INDEED FASCINATING. Just like the grand plan of the Universe and our God, we will change when we are ready to receive. This is a memoir of a soul journey. In the simplest of terms, a soul journey is a search for oneself. This isn't just a search for an aspect of oneself or direct answers to why our lives have turned out the way they have. It's a quest to understand *all* aspects of ourselves, the entirety of who we are. This means we have to understand the Divine to a much greater extent than we do now. We are each a piece of God. We have been given so many gifts, powerful gifts, but we lost the memory of them. There is a calling at this time for all of us to get back in touch with our divine soul. The lives we have been leading for a couple of dozen centuries and how we have been living these lives is unsustainable. The biggest clue that this is happening is the unhappiness and fear and sense of victimhood many of us are experiencing right now, and we don't know why we are feeling this way. For some, the only way to ease this pain is to search for answers.

"When it is time for something new, you will feel it. You will feel a desire to let go, to shed layers, to move, to recreate. You will know because there will be subtle shifts around you. You will release the old because you are really clearing the path for what's ahead. Trust this process. Know that life

does not take from us anything unless there is something else imminently awaiting its replacement."

—Brianna Wiest

There are other events that might set off a soul journey, other than the state of our world. Many of these are personal events that are big enough to wake us up and make us pay attention. Serious illness, a devastating loss, a life-changing experience . . . any one can be the final tipping point toward self-discovery. There are some blessed souls who do not have to experience a traumatic event to take this trip. They are born knowing what they need to do. Many of these people become our guides, our leaders, and our teachers. They can point out the way. I have been on two soul journeys, the one described in this book and one I embarked upon a decade earlier that I didn't even recognize as a soul journey. Not all soul journeys are spiritual, but they are effective nonetheless. Of course the most powerful ones are those where we are in partnership with the Divine . . . so much faster!

Both of my soul journeys were triggered by suffering and/or deep unhappiness. The first one was a response to the pervasive unhappiness (not depression) I experienced as a result of a difficult and traumatic childhood. The second one came as a result of the death of our eighteen-year-old son, Patrick, in 2003.

It was Patrick's sudden and unexplained death that led me on a final quest for answers. Why did he die? How did I fit into this scenario? What was my influence in his life that led him to make the choices he did? What is the grand scheme of things? So many questions! There was so much I didn't know but knew that I had to learn. I explored my son's life through his journals to see exactly the part I played. This was just one aspect of the trip I took. Studying his life the way I did helped me to understand mine. The rest of what I had to learn was all on me!

It had been decades since I last explored the metaphysical aspects of spirituality, meta-science, religion, and similar modalities. As a teenager, I was extremely attracted to the metaphysical . . . tarot cards, astrology, mediums, channelers, Edgar Cayce, and more. I was enthralled with the statements of power we hold, and I wanted to access all of them. At the time, however, metaphysics was not considered a science, and none of the powers it promised were provable.

I had a big surprise in store the second time around. Science had been busy while I was doing other things. It wasn't long before I discovered that advances in the field of quantum physics, medicine, and epigenetics, et al., seemed to be one breath away from information I had gleaned from the purely metaphysical work I was involved with years prior. At that time, the division between science and the metaphysical was a chasm as wide as the Grand Canyon. Today, the differences look more like a stick in the sand. In contrast to the early days, I discovered the science of today supports and substantiates much of the metaphysical. Armed with this information, I felt like I had finally been given permission to explore these realms to my heart's delight. Knowing the science-metaphysical connection gave me the courage to continue on.

As I was learning, I could see concepts and ideas organizing themselves into related categories. After a time, I started to recognize these categories as truths for me. As I applied these truths to my daily life, I realized I was creating a new matrix of life for myself, and the truths I came across would be the new anchor points. I realized I was uncovering a whole new me. I was on the threshold of a new beginning! A chapter is devoted to each of the six truths I adopted as my blueprint for transformation and shows how I applied them to my life.

Soul journeys don't always follow a straight line. When we take to books, we are downloading a lot of information. I found it interesting that the information that "stuck" to me was exactly what I needed to move ahead at the time. My son's story follows in linear time, but it was important that I understood my role in his life to really understand mine. You will find his story woven into the truths I selected. Sometimes a particular truth will add important information to what happened in his life, sometimes it doesn't seem to be related, so forgive me for that. It may be hard to imagine, but at the end of the day, *everything* is connected.

As I put Patrick's story to words, I am impressed with a point of view flooding my senses that doesn't seem to be mine. I know this voice! I recognize it! I came to realize that portions of what I was writing were coming from my son! Apparently, he decides to weigh in from an elevated point of view I don't possess. Excited to have him on the team, I name these welcome interruptions *Heavenly Hindsights*. They begin each chapter.

The work with my son's journals, the study of new modalities of information, the inspiration afforded me by the *Heavenly Hindsights* and my new work with personal meditation led me to the six truths that became the cornerstones for my journey. Finally, I found a path that would lead me to the joy and happiness I know I have a right to experience. The hard part has been and continues to be the application of all of this knowledge in a practical way to continue changing *how* I am.

Note, I didn't say *who* I am.

All of us are already beautiful, living souls full of love who just need a tiny makeover . . . out with old attitudes and beliefs and in with the new! We will finally recover our true shining selves hidden under dirt and grime for a couple of dozen centuries or even millennia. Right now, it's time to clean the jewels!

> *"The Spiritual Journey is individual, highly personal. It can't be organized or regulated. It isn't true that everyone should follow one path. Listen to your own Truth."*
>
> **—Ram Dass**

Yes, soul journeys are extremely unique and extremely personal. There is no one path or one way. There is, however, one objective

. . . and that is to return to Source, our God, and that will require a lot of love. How we get there is up to us. My story is an example of what *one* soul journey can look like. The information on the truths I offer might be of keen interest to some since many of these ideas are rather grand and powerful. If something resonates, we might explore, and as we explore, we will discover. It is inspiration that often gets to us and keeps us going. I have found my own search to have been extremely meaningful. A new me is emerging, and I never knew she existed! What an adventure!

The Agreement

I LEFT THE CLASSROOM with the other souls in a high state of excitement. We had just had a wonderful master class in energy manipulation for the purpose of creating a device that would collect beneficial intentions and store them individually as beads on a string. The point is to see if this heavenly bracelet can incarnate with souls on earth and serve as remedies or reminders of the challenges they will face. It's been a fun project, but it needs a bit of work. The contents of the beads can only be accessed with pure love and compassion, which will require the wearer to actually use these heavenly personality traits. As always, the condition of the spirit in the human body is the wild card. We are constantly working to help those incarnated on the other side to eventually find their way home. These souls are all we think about until it is our time to return.

As my energy sphere floated out the room, I was, as usual, awed and amazed by the incredible beauty of the others as we exited together. Some were a brilliant white, so bright and pure that it should have been painful. Others wore dazzling pink with flecks of gold that drove the heart to pure love. Others still wore perfect blues, silvers, ambers, and yellows with various threads of complementary colors woven throughout. My own sphere is amber with sparkles of pink and surrounded by an aura of blue, which signifies my impending incarnation. If I wasn't already in "heaven," I would have recognized these as heaven's colors, for such perfection could never be found on earth. Further, each energy sphere is distinguished by one single perfect tone of sound. No one has the same tone. The sound vibrations are as different as they can be from each other, but all are 100 percent harmonious.

I was on my way to the Life Planning Zone where I would put the finishing touches on the next incarnation I have been working on with my Soul Group. This was to be an important meeting. My guides, angels, master guides, and certain soul family members would be waiting for me there. We had been at this for a while.

There is a great deal of planning that goes into preparing each soul for its next incarnation. There is so much enthusiasm and love from not only those who will be participating in the development of my plan, but from those who will be joining me in life. I, however, am the only one who can decide what it is I will ultimately choose. That is my right.

Throughout all of our lives, our primary concern, as we are motivated to create new life, is karma. Karma is not punishment, as so many on earth believe. Rather, it is a correction . . . an "adjustment" of energy that has created an imbalance in the perfect order of things. Karma is a word that describes the activity, energy, creation, and struggle involved in bringing things back to order. Its concept is entwined in lessons and the new knowledge and wisdom that we receive as a byproduct of our efforts. Karma is a good thing. It's just not an easy thing.

I had already decided that this next lifetime will be the one to finally balance the karmic conditions I created in several prior lifetimes. For one reason or another, I was unable to redeem the negative effects of certain actions and thoughts I struggled with in other lives. When this state exists, karma builds over time, and the earthly lessons become more difficult. I had definitively already decided that in this next life I would learn what I needed to learn once and for all!

The soul, Delvael, aka Patrick, is to play a significant role in my next life. He and I have been together many times before. We have been brother and sister, father and son, teacher and student, employer and employee, slave owner and slave . . . we have shared many lives. He is one of my favorite soul group members, and I'm so glad he agreed to participate with me. He, himself, has some karmic energy that also needs to be cleared, and both he and I determined that, with the plan we put together, both of us will have the chance to clear all of this and move forward in our development.

We put together a plan and shook on it. We had an Agreement, and we both were determined to honor it, despite the difficulties of doing so on earth. This is the story of that agreement and what came of it.

CHAPTER ONE

Setting the Stage

Heavenly Hindsight

(3.3.3). MARCH 3, 2003. That was my day to die. Of course, I didn't know it at the time, but that was the very second in the ordained scheme of things the infinite universe set aside for me to die. That second was for me and me alone, which, if you think about it, is pretty mind boggling. Think of all the lives that have lived before you, all life not only on this earth but throughout our universe and other universes. It is truly significant to have a piece of it devoted just to you. For I know now that in the second of my death, the sum total of all that I was and all that I did and all those that I touched in my living time came full circle. From my death I came to know the enormous meaning and purpose of who I am and how I expressed myself in this life. I came to know how my life culminated from all that came before and would contribute to all that was to come. Perfect. The universe is perfect in balance. Nature is balanced. Nature is energy. I am energy. Cause and effect. Every action is balanced by reaction. Balance. Perfect balance.

I am Patrick, aka Delvael. I am the soul Mom was talking about at the beginning of this story and with whom I had made the agreement of a lifetime. Like all other souls that choose earth as their divine classroom, I also had a journey to make in my short time here. There was a certain specific karma I had to address in order to finalize the lessons I had been working on for several incarnations. This karma had been hanging around far too long, and I knew the longer I took to address it, the harder it would get. The decision my mom and I made together for our mutual benefit was a tough one, but we both agreed that it was necessary for the two of us to complete this particular phase of soul development.

Here on the "Other Side" we can see and understand truth and all of its aspects. We know how it all fits together. We don't have this advantage while in human form, but it is incumbent on us to search for it anyway and learn to understand it.

When I passed away and was on my way to True Home, I knew I had succeeded! I had been so close in prior lifetimes to clearing my karmic imbalance. I just needed one more pass to get it right. It wasn't necessary to live out a full human lifetime to accomplish what I needed to get done.

When I arrived home, I found I had been elevated to the level of Teaching Soul! It was in this capacity that I helped Mom write this book.

Of course, I didn't know I was going to die on March 3, 2003. I was eighteen . . . almost nineteen. I was a guy, a stud actually, pretty damn cool if you really want to know. I was in my prime as a first-year college student. I had Joanne, my first and only love, in my life, and my mom bought me a Chico State matching sweat jacket and sweatpants outfit I just had to have.

She had come to visit me a few weeks before I died, and we shopped the student store. She was in a buying mood for me, and I definitely wanted to accommodate her. I saw the outfit. It was something I could never afford, but I liked it. My mom thought it was kind of dorky, you know the kind of thing the "ultra-preps" would wear. But I saw "cool." Even Joanne laughed at me when I wore it. I have to admit, it was a bit out of my style, a complete change, but damn! I liked it. And I wore it . . . no . . . I posed in it

. . . casually leaning on a campus building with cell phone in hand waiting for Joanne's class to end. She would crack up when her class was over, and I would laugh with her, but you know, that outfit was my statement of what I was at that moment in time and the final portrait of everything that had come before. It was good.

A lot of me had been changing just prior to my death. I can see that now, of course, but then I just felt different. I felt anxious, sometimes irritable. I had a nagging sense of urgency that I just couldn't shake. Normally I move about kind of slow, not sluggish slow, but slow in a deliberate kind of way. It was part of that "cool" I had been working on all through my high school years and before. It was my signature and a good style for me. It worked because I had the physicality to carry it off . . . tall, very lean, dark almost black hair and eyes.

My dad is of Czechoslovakian and Norwegian origin and is a very quiet, reflective person. The quiet on him makes him a very interesting person because he is also extremely intelligent. You just want to know what he is thinking. I could carry off that same mystery and draw people to me in the same way, but I got a bonus from my mom. I liked to talk. I liked to watch people and try to figure out who they were, their motivations, what they wanted, why they did what they did.

Girls, especially, liked this quality in me, because, well frankly, girls just love to analyze people. Unlike my mom, however, I was very selective in who I shared my talking gift with. Frankly, I had to pick and choose who that would be. I found most people unable to appreciate the weight of what I might want to say, so I could be arrogant and dismissive.

But I sure as hell liked having these folks around, so I worked Dad's mysterious side of me to keep them interested. I have to admit, it didn't require nearly as much effort as the talking thing did.

In the weeks before I died, however, I found myself jittery, anxious, talking way too fast . . . almost breathless. It was weird. It was unsettling. Something was up. I was also getting headaches and chest pains. Bad chest pains. I thought it was indigestion. My mom told me it was indigestion, so I took Tagamet. The pains would go away and I was good, except for that anxious feeling. I had been getting those chest pains for a while now . . . actually, off and on since middle school. They were annoying but did go away. Lately, though, I was getting them more frequently. I was just too young for anyone to think I might have a "condition." Even I didn't know I had a "condition."

Since I currently have the advantage of looking at my life from an elevated perspective, I will take the liberty to add to the important messages of the divine truths that follow. From my perch here, I can clear up loose ends and provide new insights to what is discussed. Sometimes a dose of heavenly wisdom is helpful for humans struggling to escape the chasms of disbelief where they often find themselves trapped.

Setting the Stage

We come to earth as actors each time we incarnate. The earth is our stage, and the mask we wear this time around dictates the role we will play. We are good at what we do. We know the storyline, our motivations, and we definitely know our challenges. The play is cleverly designed with many improvisational moments for, at any given time, we can change the direction of the storyline just by the choices we make.

When the play is over, we take off our masks and return home . . . our true home. Here we can rest in grandeur with the whole of our authentic selves . . . until we are called to perform again.

For any story to be told, we must set the stage. Stories "flow" from the establishing scene. The story of my early life provides information on events that occurred and the beliefs I formed about myself and my life as a result of these events. I don't provide too much detail on the events themselves because, really, they aren't that important. What makes them important is the belief system I created around them. The attitudes I carried about myself and my place in this world from these beliefs were not what I would call "elevated." I hope to show how carrying these kinds of thoughts about ourselves, without any kind of resolution, can create great suffering. I also hope to show that we are never, ever bound by the cages we create for ourselves. We can open the door at any time and leave. We just have to want to do so.

Act I

As a child growing up in the 1950s, I had a tough life. My dad, an Air Force pilot, was killed in an aircraft accident at the age of thirty-two, leaving my mom with three young girls. Within a year, she married a young man seven years her junior . . . and she was only twenty-seven! They had three more children together. I was the oldest, then, at six. Their relationship was not a healthy one, and all of the children suffered in different ways. When my stepfather turned forty, he committed suicide, having discovered several months before that he had a form of cancer.

Mentioned earlier, I had a great attraction to the metaphysical and spent a good amount of time playing with its concepts. I also attended a Catholic girl's school for eleven years. My first indoctrination into the Catholic faith was in second grade at age seven. We had reached the Age of Consciousness and were on deck to receive the Holy Sacraments of Confession and First Communion. Perhaps I didn't get indoctrinated soon enough. As we learned the doctrines, rules, and dogma of the Catholic church, I found myself skeptical.

I was madly in love with guardian angels and was so glad to learn we all had one. I dreamed of the day when I could see her. On the other hand, this business of hell, limbo, and purgatory didn't set well with me. I thought the arrangement was too harsh. We were learning that the God in the New Testament is the God of Love. All of this punishment-based dogma didn't make me feel the love. I also took exception, yes even at age seven, that our faith was "The One True Religion." It felt so unnecessarily exclusionary. Further, my confusion over church teachings was exasperated by the kindness and compassion of the nuns who taught us. How could these people be so good and so kind and give up their life to serve God especially in light of the "threats" offered by their religion? It was conflicting and confusing at the same time. I don't do well under threat of punishment, thus making it hard to reconcile living from a heart of goodness with the "Rules of Engagement" of my faith.

I realize now that my experimentation with occult studies was my first attempt with trying to find out who I was and what I was supposed to be doing here. I kept at it for fun and thought I might be learning something. When I started having children in my thirties, I took a break. That decade was pretty much devoted to child rearing.

As I made my way to my late thirties and early forties, I was pretty unhappy with myself. The source of my unhappiness was elusive. It made little sense to me. It wasn't until I had my own children that I was able to make the connection. I experienced a spontaneous revelation that the great love I had for my own children was *not* as I remembered as a child. Confused at first, I realized that I had harbored a belief for a very long time that . . . I was just not a lovable child. I knew I could love and be loved! This was not a truth that I was prepared to accept at this time. I had been living like this for a long time. I made the commitment to change my life once and for all. I needed to fix things! I didn't have a clue as to where to start.

Act II

So I opened up my mind and allowed myself to be attracted to "remedies" that I thought might help my state of mind. After I quit my career to stay home with my children, I took the opportunity to explore the offerings from the world of art. When the kids got to school, I had several hours during the day where I could take classes, go to school, and learn.

The first order of healing for me was writing in my journal. Before the family woke up for school, I would light my candle and write for at least an hour before breakfast needed to be made. I poured my heart out in those journals. *Everything* went in there. I needed to see my pain in words. I did this for three years.

My greatest personal challenge at the time was my fear of rejection. I decided to face this fear by enrolling in an acting class. I surmised that actors get nothing but rejection, especially when auditioning, so if I couldn't cure this by going to auditions, nothing would help. I studied, auditioned, and acted in commercials and independent film for eight years. I didn't worry much about rejection after that.

As a child, my great dream was to be a dancer. I was not encouraged in this endeavor. Rather, I was told I am "good with my hands" and should focus there. Unable to draw any link between good hands and a potential career at the time, I dismissed the suggestion and enrolled in jazz, modern dance, and contemporary dance classes. It wasn't until I finally started ballet that I had found my match. Until we made our move to a new state last year, I spent twenty-five wonderful years in the studio.

When my daughter picked up the violin in third grade, I decided to take lessons with her. The teacher wouldn't let me wait out my daughter's thirty-minute lesson in her house, and I didn't want to sit in a hot car on the driveway, so I signed up to take lessons with her. As is often (sadly) the case with adults learning an entirely new skill, I was never very good at the violin. My daughter advanced so quickly in terms of skill and talent that I had to back off taking lessons with her. I was holding her back. Still, I continued and managed to lock down fourteen years of playing. This included a three-year stint as a second violinist in the community college symphony orchestra and ten years as a member of a piano quartet.

Writing, acting, dancing, and music! What wonderful ways to open one's heart! In retrospect, I realize the time I spent pursuing my love for the arts can be viewed as a soul journey of sorts. It truly did change me. After ten years, I emerged full of confidence in myself and my accomplishments. I was starting to like myself. My physical appearance changed. Unable in the beginning to lose the extra weight from my second pregnancy, I joined Weight Watchers. In one month, I had lost thirteen pounds. Then I started my ballet classes. Afterward and unbeknownst to me, I continued to lose about two pounds a year. By the end of the decade, I was down a total of thirty pounds, which put me at my fighting weight! As someone who had fought a lifetime battle with weight, I had shed all that poundage, and I didn't even notice. I was having too much fun! I also found myself consistently happy for the first time in my life. And when I found myself in a happy state, I found so many others living in joy.

This was indeed a soul journey. It did help me uncover my artistic side, which was a wonderful, fulfilling feeling. I knew I was getting closer to the core of who I really was. I still had much "inside" work to do, but at the time, I didn't know it. Later, upon reflection, I realize the missing ingredient to this effort was the connection to the Divine. This was not a spiritual quest, but it was the way I was going to have to travel to really get to the heart of my troubles.

Act III

The day Patrick died, despite the temporary insanity of the family members left behind just after getting the bad news, I felt a sense of relief woven throughout the tears and gut-wrenching grief. I hated this feeling! It seemed so selfish and mean. Why did I feel relief? He was on such a good path. He had succeeded in overcoming his demons and was happier than he had ever been. Relief?!! I did not understand this reaction and kept it to myself. It wasn't normal from my point of view.

When he passed, I felt oddly detached from everything. This wasn't on an obvious level as there was much to do in the hours and days just after he died. It was as if the claws of hopeless grief or guilt or anger did not touch me too terribly close. I had no regrets. Yes, I was unbelievably sad. I would miss him so much. I was so proud of him. It's just this detachment seemed so odd. At the same time, however, I was secretly grateful that I didn't have to fully experience the depths that grief and loss usually reveal. I also found myself grateful that my son died at the top of his game! I thought about this a lot over the following weeks. Even today, I believe my overwhelming gratitude for the life he led carried me through the worst of what I had yet to experience.

The days and weeks following Patrick's death were chaotic. I cannot fully express the appreciation I have for my family, who all rallied and came to us in the middle of the night we got the call. Again, bathing in gratitude for their support and love, I found the feeling pervasive. I seemed to be grateful about everything.

The funeral held at the Catholic church in town drew over five hundred people. I noticed this always seems to happen when a young person dies. I have no idea how many people came to the house, but there were a lot. I glided over all the proceedings in an altered state. I see photos of the event, and I look so serene and peaceful. I don't know why. In the months that followed, I wrote a personal note to every single person who attended the service or helped out or even sent a card. I was incredibly busy with minutiae . . . thank God! It saved my sanity, especially through those first few raw months following his death.

Messages From the Other Side

Despite my fascination with the metaphysical, I haven't had much prior experience with metaphysical events or messages or visions . . . except when I imagined it. After my son passed, I became aware of a big one . . . the Premonition of all Premonitions. It happened on the day Patrick was born.

I recall gazing at my firstborn in his crib next to me in the hospital room. He was so beautiful, and he looked so much like my husband. Like many parents must experience at some point in time, I was in awe of the miracle sleeping so soundly next to me. As I was daydreaming and admiring, a thought flashed in my head that frightened and confused me. I heard only these words: *"You know, he won't be here for very long."* What the hell was that?!! That wasn't my thought! It was awful. At least on the surface, I couldn't imagine thinking anything like that after just giving birth. But there was a quality to this thought that was different. It came to me as a reminder, not to scare me, but to remind me of something.

Rather than dismissing it entirely, I recall answering this new bit of information. I said to self, *"Sixteen. I've got him till he's sixteen."* This was an absolutely nonsensical response. And I did not think this thought again or even reflect on it until sixteen years later on the morning of Patrick's birthday. It bounced right to the front of my brain, fresh as a daisy. I was reeling but tucked the thought away again. Both Pat and I survived his sixteenth year and the following year when he turned seventeen. At that time, I recall my thoughts, *"If he lives through his eighteenth year, he is mine. I will have won!"* When he turned eighteen, I went through the same ritual. In March of 2003, Patrick was just two months shy of his nineteenth birthday. I figured I had already beaten the odds, so relaxed by the time he would hit that milestone.

Joanne, Patrick's girlfriend from college, and several members of my family, had visitations from Patrick in their dreams or other creative venue choices in the months and even years after he passed . . . except me. I don't know why. I thought I might have deserved it since I was so hard on him during those last two years of high school. I was prepared to accept my fate, but I wasn't happy about it. I knew he was out there. I knew he was not gone. I knew I would have to wait. In the meantime, I took solace in others' experiences.

Patrick worked mightily to get Joanne's attention. She told me she could feel him all around her, and one time she saw him partially materialize, but it frightened her. A year or two later, when she moved away from Chico and enrolled in nursing school in San Bernardino, she would tell me of strange happenings in her apartment with lights and electricity. Both of us would have chalked up the experience as a result of an overactive, wishful-thinking mind had it not been for Joanne's roommate. A fellow nursing student, this young man started to complain about the lights turning on and off, both while he was home and when he returned home.

In the years that followed, I always made it a point to do something special for Patrick on his birthday and his death day. Most of the time, I would write a letter or a poem or a story, but I was diligent. I also tried to make sure my husband and daughter remembered. It didn't take long for me to realize that I didn't have to continue nagging either one of them to take the time to remember. Patrick, himself, let his displeasure be known. My husband is a computer guy, just like Patrick and everyone else on his side of the family. I will never forget the first time he forgot Patrick's birthday. He had been using Patrick's rebuilt computer for one aspect of his digital media business and went to work the morning of Pat's birthday. He went downstairs to his studio and found the computer screen open with random words displayed in sixty+ font. I was the only one living at home at the time, so I didn't do it! My husband knew of only one complicated way of making this bizarre display, but it would require human assistance. He asserted there was *no way* this could have happened on its own. And it didn't. It was Patrick.

Patrick always let us know he was there by messing with the technology. On other missed dates, computers crashed or malfunctioned in some bizarre yet benign way. Cell phones went dead. All of the problems were resolved within a few hours and all on their own. Both my husband and daughter didn't need to hear from me why this happened, but they never let it happen again.

For a while, my feelings were a little hurt that everyone else was getting messages. After all, I have always been the "metaphysical" one in the family. I believed if anyone should have the recipient of an "experience," it should have been me. I was most open to the idea!

It was six years before I had my own Patrick experience. I remember the day so well. It was a gorgeous, warm, breezy Indian summer day. I was running errands around town. All the windows in the car were open . . . I hate air conditioning. I was calm and content and not thinking about anything in particular. As I was driving, I noticed a wonderfully, oddly blissful warmth enveloping my body. This was a completely different kind of warm than that of the weather. This warmth felt alive! That is my best shot at explaining it. I felt so peaceful, so happy, and then I glanced over to the passenger side and there he was! In my mind's eye, I saw my beautiful son sitting next to me with the windows open and the wind blowing through his hair. He was leaning back in the seat with his eyes closed and his elbow resting on the windowsill. He was nodding his head as if listening to his favorite song on the radio. (This was often his pose when we toodled around together running errands.) Finally! I was overjoyed. I had never felt that kind of warmth before. I knew this was real and was satisfied I was now part of the club.

My Son, the Teacher?

Sometime after Patrick died and things had calmed down a bit, my husband and I decided to visit a medium. We wanted to know how he died. The cause of death on the autopsy report stated, "undetermined, natural causes." His death was sudden and spontaneous, and the autopsy report disclosed no medical issues whatsoever. It was a mystery, but we had to know. In my opinion, there is nothing natural about an eighteen-year-old suddenly ceasing to exist.

At the time, we were members of Compassionate Friends, a support group for those who have lost their children. Karen Petersen, our psychic, offered pro-bono readings to this particular group of parents as her way of giving back. When she was ready to channel Patrick, she began by sharing bits of information about him. This was to help validate for her that this was indeed our son we would be talking to. The first thing we asked him was how he died. In response, Karen placed her hand over her heart and said the problem was with his heart. It was an undetectable defect he had had since birth. It was just one of those inexplicable events. His heart just quit on him . . . at eighteen years of age. Somewhat comforted that he didn't die from any mind-altering substances, we settled in to hear what else he had to say.

He wanted us to give a message to a friend of his. Sam was a few years older than Patrick so didn't hang around with his usual crowd. Somehow they connected at an event through high school and became pretty tight. I believe Patrick looked up to him like an older brother. The message Patrick asked us to deliver, through Karen, was, *"Do NOT marry her!"* At first, I couldn't imagine who he was talking about. All the friends I could think of were only eighteen years old, just like Patrick, and way too young for marriage. Karen tried to help out by giving us initials of a name she was receiving. My husband and I flashed on Sam, who was about twenty-three at the time. In the most coincidental of meetings, Sam had come to our house a couple of weeks before just to check in and see how we were doing. He brought a young woman with him and introduced her as his fiancée. He was deliriously happy. There was *no* way I was going to deliver that message! I did decide, however, to keep tabs on him, so we became Facebook friends. He eventually married the girl, and things seemed to be going pretty well. It was about a year later that I learned he had divorced! I couldn't believe it. I learned later that sometimes our lost loved ones will use an example like this one just to prove to us that they are not gone! They are with us always.

As our reading was wrapping up, Karen said Patrick had one more thing he wanted to tell us. He was quite proud that he had been assigned the role of "Teacher" on the other side. Now this information really attracted my attention. Since when did Heaven have teachers and how is it my son is one of them? I had no knowledge of anything having to do with an afterlife, except that which I was taught in the church . . . and no one ever mentioned heavenly teachers. It would be many years into the future before I had the answer, but at the time, I knew it was a profound piece of information.

I was fifty years old when Patrick passed away. As I look back on the things I did to find happiness, I concluded that the previous ten years of work I did to heal myself was absolutely critical to prepare me for the challenge of my son's death. I thought I was healing my past, and I was, but I was really preparing myself for the future. The work I did strengthened me physically, mentally, and emotionally. It was necessary to withstand what was coming my way. After Patrick died and a little time had passed, I again became dissatisfied with my life. Losing a child should not be my defining life's purpose. I had already been through so much. It just didn't make sense to me that we could suffer so in the time we are alive only to find there is no obvious meaning or purpose behind this suffering.

Finding meaning then, finding purpose was at the heart of my unhappiness this time around. I had so many questions, and I craved answers. So, after a twenty-year hiatus, I dug up my old astrology charts, books, and tarot cards and starting asking new and different questions. Also at my disposal were new discoveries from the science world that hinted of a scientific connection to a divine universe. There were new cards, such as Oracle cards and Past Life cards, that offered newer and fresher insights than the Tarot. I had access to so much new material and was developing an interesting and new relationship with science and metaphysics. I needed to read and learn. This was the stirring of a spiritual soul journey about to make its debut. I would be in for quite a ride. There are many truths to learn. Knowledge, however, is only one part of the equation. Once we know what we need to know, we must learn how to apply these divine laws to our daily lives. It is only in the application of wisdom to our daily lives that we can grow, heal, and transform. We need to walk the walk. We need to show how we believe.

The Creation of a Soul Journey

Questions are the building blocks of soul journeys. We want to know why something happened. We want to know why we are unhappy. We want to know why we seem to attract so much sadness to our lives. For me, it was the "why" questions that kickstarted my quest. "Why" questions can begin vaguely and eventually crystallize into something more specific or they can just appear at the front of your consciousness demanding an answer. They appear so that they can be answered. This is our call to do something.

Knowing how to ask for help from God or other divine sources starts with knowing what you want to know. There is an advantage to getting old. There is nothing a few decades of living can't do to make us more in touch with who we truly are. As I mature, I notice my questions are more specific and directed. Unfortunately, we live in a culture that chooses to view wisdom as a side effect of a long life rather than the tool it is to understand why we have to live this life at all. I have different questions now than I did when I was in my twenties.

The approach I took and the process I engaged in to get some of these answers was rather random and a bit all over the place. Nevertheless, I somehow managed to hit on the important things I needed to know to get started. I simply gravitated to what I was attracted to at the time. Some days I wrote. Some days I read. Some days I meditated. Some days I did it all. This was my beginning. After a time, everything sorted itself out and morphed into an "official" practice.

Meditation

"Now you may call this a spiritual or psychological or psychic exploration as you prefer . . . There are far more wonders to be achieved through this inward exploration than you can possibly believe."

—Seth

Meditation has proven to be the most effective tool in my toolbox. But I needed to know things first, so I spent the lion's share of time reading. This seemed like a wise choice because meditation can be confusing if you don't understand how it works. If one is on a soul quest, knowledge moves the process along very quickly. If one just wants to meditate to relax or feel good, that works too, but we accomplish so much more when we have a plan in mind and know who and how to ask for help. There are many, many meditation protocols. When I started exploring, I needed to learn the purpose of the styles I was considering. Some practices are for very specific outcomes. To date, I've only explored the tip of the iceberg, but needing something new at this time isn't necessary. I have switched approaches depending on where I am in my journey, and my practice today is working just fine. I also know that when I have reached a new spiritual level, I will feel the urge to explore a new modality again. It's all part of the process.

The best side effect of regular meditation is how good I feel most of the day. Many troubling physical aches and pains have diminished . . . significantly. I truly carry a sense of peace and calm throughout the day. I notice how I can face most daily challenges now with greater composure. And I am getting answers! At first, this information would come to me in pieces without apparent reason or explanation. Sometimes, they would come without context, making it difficult to know what to do. I felt like I was learning a different language, and I guess I was, having had no real experience with talking to God directly. I do know, however, that the information I receive always seems to be related to the bigger effort of trying to piece this life of mine together. The answers eventually reveal themselves when I least expect it and only when I can understand. It's a beautiful process.

This is the way of the Divine. We attract what we need the most. My story of the truths that follow show the path of knowledge I selected for my growth and evolution. By studying this information, I was able to clear bad attitudes, determine what my dreams and ambitions were telling me and, as a result, have come that much closer to understanding my purpose in life and the meaning behind it. Everyone's path is as different as there are truths out there. The six truths I identify become the cornerstones for my personal journey. There are so many more, but these are mine. Let's begin.

CHAPTER TWO

The Subject of Truths

Heavenly Hindsight

I WAS AWARE THAT my "soon to be" mom on the earthly plane would call me to her planning meeting. I was also not surprised. We had had so many successful past earthly lives together that it seemed appropriate that she would call on me to participate in this next one for herself. I had to think about it for a little while because I, myself, have been in the process of planning my own incarnation. Timing was an issue since the life I have been planning would not be scheduled until much later. Certain events must occur for me to be able to clear my karma. The time frames for my life's plan and my mom's plan did not cleanly match up.

Nevertheless, I felt compelled to attend. I was sure something could be worked out. The planning session itself is a wondrous affair. There are so many souls in attendance. Most of them will have a part in my mom's life. Some of those roles will be quite large, others may last just a moment in time, but all are important for the choreography to manifest. No one is dispensable.

When I entered the planning arena, there were dozens and dozens of attendees. Planning sessions are a lot like earthly cocktail parties where everyone is in a fine mood. Our cocktail of choice is massive amounts of love, and many were drunk from its effects.

My mom was sitting in the middle of the room. She was surrounded by her guides, teachers, protective angels, and master guides. In the middle of the circle around which they gathered was a flat board that looked like a giant gaming table. This wonderful creation was multi-dimensional, with any number of twin boards hovering over the main board. The game pieces were the individuals and characters, events and places that needed to be placed in just the right spot at just the right time for something to occur. The "something" expected to occur was generally the catalyst for a massive transformation being planned. When I arrived, game pieces were flying from one board to another. This was for the purpose of viewing how one occurrence will lead to another and how, in the long run, the final outcome will be affected.

In a planning session, there is much discussion on the topics of lessons, karma, and agreements. There is much, much more, of course, but these topics are so prevalent they are imbedded in our earthly memories. Somehow, we arrive on the earthly plane with a strong sense that we have a purpose there. As we live our lives, we learn to recognize that what happens on earth can easily fall into one or all of the above categories. It is an easy way to help us remember and learn.

Mom touched on karma in the prologue. I have a word or two to say about lessons and agreements.

Lessons are *not* punishment. There is nothing bad about lessons. Lessons, which can manifest in an infinite number of ways, should always be considered A Gift! There are times when we get so wrapped up in our earthly lives that we forget why we are there. A lesson does two things: 1) It slows us down so that we finally do find the time to think about things, and 2) It serves to point us back to the path of the plan we originally created and to which we agreed.

Sometimes lessons manifest in the form of illness. Illness is a major wake-up call that signals the need to slow down, stop even, and reflect on how we got there. We don't plan for illness or death in the heavenly plane. We plan specifically for healing. Illness, as a lesson then, is more of a red light than a yellow light. It is a massive wake-up call, i.e. an opportunity to change something!

Agreements are the pacts made between souls to help insure a necessary event will occur. Some events are tragic, some are joyful, and some are just shocking. Why would anyone plan for any one of these things, except for maybe Joy?

There is much speculation in the earthly plane as to the true role of murderer, rapist, tyrant, alcoholic, thief, and more. Sadly, the deeds done by certain perpetrators are viewed as evil, horrific, unspeakable, and unimaginable. Suspend disbelief for a second and consider…just consider…that if it were not for the dastardly deeds of others, we wouldn't have Saints, Heroes, Saviors, or the like.

What of these perpetrators? They too are children of the Great Light, the Divine, and they too are deeply loved. When they agree to commit a horrific act in the life plan of another, they are agreeing out of great, great love. This comes from a deep connection to their planning partner so that his soul can experience redemption.

You'll just have to take my word for it that the soul that "gets to play the bad guy" is also getting something out of the deal. This generally has to do with *their* plan and the path they must take to earn their place at God's side. There is no chaos or disorder on the other side. Everything happens for a reason. And *all* will eventually find their true place with the Divine.

When I was called to the center of the room, my spirit arrived dressed in a veil that hinted of my earthly appearance. I had been trying on different looks and had decided on a young male with an easy look and demeanor. Mom's lesson was a big one. The more we overlook our karmic debts in past lives, the harder the lessons yet to come will be. Karma must be balanced one way or another!

I agreed to Mom's plan, but with one caveat. It would be necessary for me to leave her at a young age in order for me to keep my appointment with my next incarnation. We figured it was a good agreement for the both of us. Mom wasn't happy about the idea of my leaving so soon, but she agreed out of great love for herself and for me. The part I will play in her life will also positively affect how I will handle the challenges yet to come for me. [1]

The Subject of Truths

I was excited to get going! As is usually the case when I approach something new, I imagine the best possible outcome, and I imagine myself achieving this result right away. When will I learn? Nothing is ever as easy as I imagine. There are always caveats. And so it was as I began to explore. At the time, of course, I didn't know I was on a search for truths. I just thought if I did what I learned I was supposed to be doing, I would have answers, experiences, Kundalini moments, and instant growth. There was knowledge that I needed to be acquainted with before any discussion of a divine universal truth could be engaged. I needed to know the basics first. This level of information was delivered first and before I became aware of the truths that would eventually guide my life.

My Journey to Understand

The Illusions of Three-Dimensional Life

We have chosen earth as our playground. This is a pretty big deal. There are many, many species of life in our multi-universe system. Most of them do not choose to live out their lives on earth. Why? Earth is a harsh place to evolve! We live in a three-dimensional world that is defined by separation, duality, and time. Our environment is physically denser than that of most other planets. From the metaphysical world, I learn our planet is one of the most difficult places to learn lessons and therefore transform. Because of this, however, our environment gives us the opportunity to evolve that much faster than others. Our challenges are greater. We enter our world with built-in obstacles, and 3D living is one of them. The spiritual path doesn't really concern itself with built-in obstacles, however. We are still charged with fulfilling our purpose. It helps then to consider the following aspects of 3D living as illusions. From the universal perspective, they are illusions, since much of universal life doesn't operate from our particular set of game rules. It is a little easier on other planets or dimensions. [2]

Separation

We live in physical bodies. We also feel so very alone. In true fact, all life in the universe is intricately connected. We are all from Source (God), so this is a natural conclusion. We are connected, yes, but we must learn how to feel that connection because we have this body to deal with. Unlike other life forms, we use our bodies to learn about our lives and our world, and it is the emotions we are constantly experiencing that inform us. So our ability to experience anything on earth takes a diversion through the physical/emotional world. Feelings come to us as information about what we may have just experienced. We have to work through our emotions to connect to others. We have to work through our emotions to find our true self. We have to work through emotions to experience the joy of ascending our lives to be closer to God. This concept of separation is one reason humanity has long believed we are the only inhabitants of a multi-universe system. It wasn't until recently that we have finally opened up to the possibility of different lives elsewhere. [3]

Duality

Because we are separate and need emotion to inform us, we exhibit a much wider range of emotional response than most. We think in terms of black and white, good and evil, hot and cold, up and down.

We can be on the high of all highs or find ourselves in the pit of hell. Duality is intense. On other realms, most things are perceived in shades of gray, so any emotional effect is significantly diminished. On earth, our emotional array is vast. This gives us the unique ability to feel quite deeply. This is a wonderful and unique way to experience the glories of the Divine. We feel so much more! We must caution ourselves, however, that as we perceive events and experiences in absolutes the way we do, it makes it more difficult to be open to possibility and new creation. We must take care not to get caught up in this.

Time

I was most interested to learn that time, itself, is really an illusion. Time is not much of a concept beyond the earthly plane. Science has taken a keen interest in the subject and has learned that there are few places where life is defined with a beginning, a middle, and an end. From Dolores Cannon's book, *The Convoluted Universe: Book One* [4], I learned that the past, present, and future all exist simultaneously. We can and do *have* access to past lives, events, and people. (This is covered in the section on Reincarnation coming up.) Even more exciting, we have the ability to visit future probabilities as well. Nostradamus demonstrates this through his predictions of future events several hundred years ahead of his time.

The problem with humans is, again, the struggle with separation and duality. We forget that we are spiritual beings. Death is simply a transition from one form to another. We live on. It is sad to think that there are humans out there who think this life is it. This is all there is. Live, work, die. No purpose, no point. I don't find this type of existence meaningful at all. I'm so glad I have taken the stress of time off the table. It makes everything so much easier.

Consciousness

What is consciousness? The term has been thrown around in so many different ways it took me forever to really understand. Consciousness is more than just "being awake." Rather, it is the sum total of everything we have experienced, every thought we have ever had, every word ever spoken, every deed we have ever done, and everything we have ever believed not just in this life, but in every life we have ever led. We carry a library of information inside our subconscious. Everything we need to know about ourselves rests in our heart. This is the reason that metaphysics and even religions challenge us to "go inside" for answers. We are constantly looking for some outside person or experience to help us validate our lives. We don't have to look to anyone or have a unique experience to get our answers. We hold all the answers we need. [5]

To demonstrate this point, the world of metaphysics introduces us to the Akashic Records. Since the universe holds all data, all possibility, and is infinite in scope and is *organized*, it stands to reason there must be a repository of sorts where all of this data is held. There is. It is called the Akashic Records, and every deed, every thought, every word is recorded there. These records actually exist in a different dimension. This library holds information for our personal use and also for much grander reasons. It is available to all universal life. The value of preserving personal experiences like this is that it permanently records each individual experience of Source through our efforts. This is why we are here . . . as a vehicle for Source to experience life. Through a spiritual practice, we have opportunities to view our record now, while we are alive here on earth. We have been granted access and can access this realm through meditation and either a "human" guide or a spiritual one. [6]

"Consciousness is what gives the brain life. It is the unseen aspect of self, both aware and unaware, both conscious and subconscious, that uses the brain to capture thoughts and

then coalesces them to create Mind . . . Our subconscious is evidence that we are part and parcel of what we call God."

—Dr. Joe Dispenza [7]

When we die on earth, only our bodies die. Who lives inside those bodies remain intact and whole, regardless of the number of lives we have led or the infinite number of experiences. In fact then, we are immortal! (This was a personal question I wondered about for many years.) There are differences, however, between who we are on earth and the *authentic* self we are in the heavenly realm. Once our consciousness is free of the imprisonment of the body and the emotions that keep us there, we can experience the uniqueness and beauty and *wholeness* that is ours alone to experience. This is our Higher Self, our Authentic Self.

The good news is we have the power to experience our glorious selves without dying. Because our consciousness holds every piece of wisdom or knowledge we have ever acquired, we can access that information *NOW* while we live. We hold everything we know about this life and all our other lives, including those in the divine plane, in our subconscious. The subconscious holds everything! We just need to make access. This is the heart of any soul journey. All of the answers are *inside*! It does take much meditative work, but it is worth it! At the time I learned this, I knew nothing about myself, except that I was unhappy, but the promise resonated. I charged ahead.

Reincarnation

Interestingly enough, the first books I was attracted to and which created a major shift in my ability to understand God and our true relationship to Him involved reincarnation. I had been interested in the topic in the past, but not interested enough to really delve. The books I was attracted to this time around were written by well-known psychiatrists who, in the course of their early work with severely troubled patients, introduce a relatively new modality to their practice . . . hypnosis. (These studies were recorded in the 1970s and 1980s.)

Originally employed to help patients uncover childhood memories that might provide answers to the root cause of some current mental dysfunctions, hypnosis offered hope as a powerful tool to access this critical information. It was during this experimentation with hypnosis that some very unusual memories were being uncovered by more than a few of their patients. Going far beyond lost childhood memories, some patients began to describe different lives they claimed to have lived millennia ago. Of particular note is the detail provided on these lives. Some patients were able to speak another language and, in some rare cases, dead languages. The detail on clothing, weather, lifestyle, and activities was stunning, especially for those investigators who took it upon themselves to verify the rich detail offered about different time periods.

Initially, the psychiatrists were taken aback by what they were hearing from their patients. It was confusing and a little alarming at first, but too fascinating to ignore. The information on a patient's past lives also appeared to be relevant to the current-day physical problems of these patients. As healers, the doctors could not ignore this information, but there were challenges. The first problem to sort out was the relationship and relevance a past life had to the patient's current medical condition. The second problem was how to deal with the psychiatric community. Past-life regression, at the time, along with hypnosis, still carried the taint of its "new age-y" beginning and a hocus-pocus allure.

It wasn't long before important connections were made between the information uncovered in a past-life regression and spontaneous healing! The results appeared to be miraculous and fairly consistent. Past-life regression could no longer be ignored as an effective healing tool! (Examples of this are covered in a later chapter.) Thank goodness for the bravery and courage of these doctors for pushing on. The most impressive healings were the physical ones, but the point of the healings was a spiritually based, emotional and mental one. The mental disorders were relieved along with their physical counterparts.

I can't imagine anyone who doesn't want to physically heal himself. This healing approach was extremely attractive to me. I definitely wanted to know more, and there are always things I want to heal. (See the bibliography for source material on reincarnation.)

Could This Be Heaven?

So, what really happens after we die? What I say below is an essay of everything I had learned so far to date on the subject. The facts behind the story are real and, again, were inspired by PLR (past-life regression) case studies. The interpretation is my own unique perception from the information I have come across and should be considered in that context. How we see things can only be shaped by what we believe.

When we die, many of us do in fact travel a tunnel of darkness with a brilliant welcoming light at the end where we may be greeted by loved ones and others who have passed before. Not every soul has this experience, but a lot do. For a time, we enter a "rehab" place where the harsh effects of a life on earth can be soothed and smoothed over with understanding and love. This is not a destination, but a stop-over place where we can peacefully acclimate to our new digs. There may be angels, teachers, guides, and other elevated spiritual beings there to help us with our recovery. It all depends on the situation. After our rehab phase is completed, we then meet with our master guides to review our prior life's work. This meeting is conducted with much, much love. It is at this time we might have an opportunity to view our akashic record. Some souls have additional meetings with ascended masters and angels. It is different for everyone. We might discuss stubborn challenges and a new way to approach them in the next incarnation. We are given the "Master Plan" for future lives. When we are finished there, we finally go to the object of our quest, our true home . . . our Soul Group. [8]

Soul Groups

There is quite a bit of order in that place called LBL (life-between-lives). A lot of what goes on there is also quite familiar. Apparently, we see other beings in human form . . . just so we can "feel" at home. In reality, everything is energy in this dimension and our true selves are a wonderful spiritual essence intimately aligned with that of God. The buildings, structures, fields, mountains, rivers, and lakes we might see there are energetic manifestations and make us feel quite comfortable. There are many other LBL locations, but these are for beings from other dimensions, planets, and galaxies. Yes! Another discovery in my learning! We are definitely *not* alone! The universe is vast and infinite, and all its critters are seeking the same thing . . . to be one with God, Source, All That Is. But I digress.

The "human" area of LBL is highly reminiscent of earth. Language, however, is by thought. This is not a world of struggle like earth is, but a world of learning and creation. Everyone has a job in the LBL. All of us have unique gifts, and we are allowed to express these gifts in as large and creative a way as we want. There is no judgment in this place. Only love. But we are there for a reason. Just like on earth, we are part of a community in the LBL. This is our soul group or soul family.

Souls that are members of a particular soul group have been part of that group for a long, long time. This is our immediate heavenly family. There are different levels of soul groups, just as there are individuals at various levels of enlightenment. The family members of a particular soul group are generally at a similar level of ascension. We are very close with our family members and tend to reincarnate with each other over and over again.

The idea that we belong to a soul group really surprised me. Later on in my journey, I learned how deeply connected we are to each other, and when I think of life on earth, I think how well we always do when we are team players working on a common good. It makes sense, then, that being connected to a team of souls who have been working with each other for eons from numerous physical incarnations and who know each other *intimately* can be of tremendous benefit. It didn't take too big of a leap in imagination to welcome this version of heaven. No one works alone. We are never alone.

Creation is the primary purpose in the LBL. From a soul group perspective, there is always a great deal of activity on identifying the challenges of earthly living and our personal challenge of knowing what we need to keep working on so that we learn the lessons presented to us. Every incarnation we have is a gift from God to get it right. We have all the time in the world to get this done. The only pressure we might experience is the desire to finally evolve past our emotional body and learn to live in one with Source. All soul group members have the same goal. It is to this end, then, that much soul group activity involves planning for future incarnations, including the selection of the roles some or all of your soul group members will play. [9]

Incarnation planning sessions are taken very seriously in the LBL. When a soul is close to its next incarnation, the activity surrounding agreements, commitments, and roles is heightened. With the proper advice of our guides, we decide what lesson we must work on in the upcoming life. The master plan we put in place and the events that will happen on earth, no matter how tragic, are what *we, ourselves, have chosen*! We are the *only* ones that can agree to a situation we believe will be beneficial to us. The God-given gift of Free Will is taken very seriously in the LBL. I apparently needed a big wake-up call prior to this particular life. I needed to create a situation that would finally make me pay attention. The death of my son would be a pretty big wake-up call. This would be *my* personal remedy.

When I learned that I am the mastermind behind the planning of my life, I was hit with a new realization. How could I ever have considered myself a "victim" in any of my earthly experiences? Every challenge I have faced was created by me and my team and *for* me. I have had and have the power to make great change. While I might disagree with the intensity of the remedy I chose for this life, I also have to believe that I determined there was no other way. I guess I was right. I am comforted somewhat by the fact that I was in a highly elevated state when I made this decision and know so much more than I can know here on earth. I trust myself enough to know this was the way.

It is also important to know that members of our soul group have to agree to play a designated role in our life. I suspect, since we are all from the same soul family, that the effort here is reciprocal with each of the players agreeing to participate in an organized way. Thus, all of us eventually benefit by each other and for each other.

There is one last impediment in front of us. After creating a wonderful, loving, grand plan in the perfection of the LBL, we finally make it here on earth . . . only to forget! What is this business of forgetfulness? Why can't we remember? Oh yeah. We live in a 3D world with all of its illusions and challenges. We can't see past our noses, much less through the veil that separates us from our divinity. Why the mystery? I only got one answer. We are here to learn lessons, and if we know the lesson ahead of time, there is nothing to learn. It wouldn't be a lesson.

What Is Truth?

Truth is not a thing. It is an essence, just like God. Truth just . . . is. There is no "content" in Truth, ever. Truth is simply a statement of existence. Nothing can qualify it because there is no content. Truth is clarity. The purest forms of Truth resonate the same way pure Love resonates. Truth, like Love, is a knowing. Where can we find Truth? We can find it in the now moment. We can find it in the abyss. We can find it in nothingness. How do we know Truth? We know it by its vibration, its resonance. We feel it.

—Inspired by Total Embodiment Meditation (TEM) protocols course

Don't get too intimidated by the quote above. It took me many months to understand even a piece of this, but at the end of the day, it *is* the best definition of truth I have come across to date. With the seed of this quote planted, there will be a day when we come back to it and will have complete understanding. Just consider it a nudge in the right direction.

Here on earth, however, we have a big problem with truth. We live in an environment of fake news, half-truths, real truths that have been dismissed as irrelevant, and lies that have been camouflaged as truth. I'm sure there are other versions. So, as mankind comes to the slow realization that we have pretty much given away a good chunk of our power of free will over the past five thousand years, we find ourselves in a rudderless boat without leaders. Truth is the great connector. Without adhesion, our will as a species continues to erode. It's time to take control again.

Despite what we think our purpose might be here on earth, we have all been endowed with a lifetime mission to 1) gain knowledge and wisdom, 2) create, 3) learn our lifetime lessons, and 4) clear our Karmic imbalances.

There are an infinite number of truths that exist in the divine realm. What good are they, however, if we don't know which ones are the most important for us? What good is knowing this information exists if we don't know how to access it or its secrets? Fortunately, these questions have an easy answer! No massive enlightenment experience is necessary . . . just our own desire to take an adventure into the world of books and find our holy grail.

The best place to start is with knowledge. As we explore and learn, we sometimes come across ideas and thoughts that just stop us in our tracks. What is it about this information that is so fascinating? Why are we so attracted to it? Pay attention!! This might be the beginning of the amazing discovery of your first personal truth. Truths always make us think. As the questions take shape in our minds and we continue to explore, we, as truth seekers, begin to circle around this treasure chest of golden nuggets. The sign that you have found your truth is 100 percent resonance. You just *know*. Do not disregard. This could be the start of your soul journey!

Throughout my research, despite the differences in topics, authors, and material, I sense overarching themes across all that I am taking in. Sometime later, I see these themes as my truths. **Lessons, Energy, Creation, Free Will, Connection and Love.** These become my guideposts to discover meaning in my life and lead me to answers I thought I would never have.

On the surface, it might appear that my truths are rather commonplace . . . nothing too fancy here. What more is there to possibly know? This is when the adventure begins! There is so much meaning hidden behind these words and so much wisdom. The universe is generous with its gifts to us, but we just don't make the time to examine and explore.

Today's the day! The time is NOW!

CHAPTER THREE

The Truth of Lessons

Heavenly Hindsight

WE BEGIN OUR LESSONS the moment we are aware of our incarnation. This can occur anywhere from four to six months after our souls join with a fetus already growing in our mothers' bodies. This time of growth can be such a wonderful, safe, warm, and loving time. We instantaneously sense the feelings and thoughts of our mothers. While this is a physical growing environment, it is also our first classroom, where we are introduced to the experience of emotion as one of the first challenges presented to us as newly incarnated beings.

Our ability to manage our emotions is one of the most important lessons of the earthly world. Our emotions, which are the byproducts of a thought or experience, are ground zero for the foundation upon which our earthly lives will be built. How well we love, how well we *are* loved, how healthy we are, how creative we are, and how well we fulfill our purpose in this life begin with how we feel and demonstrate our emotions.

Mom went back to work six weeks after I was born. As an infant, I loved her being around. I loved the sound of her voice and her laugh. And then she was gone. I was being handled by strangers, and because there were others of my ilk needing attention, my cries were not always answered right away. My infant daycare was about a half mile from the office where Mom worked. Her hours were very long, however, and we had a forty-five-minute drive home. She had little time for me when we did get home because I needed to be cleaned up, fed, and she had to make dinner for herself and Dad. Then I was put down for the night. I felt abandoned.

Even as an infant, the impressions and feelings we take in begin to shape us. Though my mom loved me very much, she made the choice to go back to work. She wanted me to have an advantage. I knew this, of course, before I incarnated, but it didn't deaden the effect of abandonment post-incarnation. I chose to accept this challenge and, thusly, experienced my first earthly lesson.

Because I knew my time in this life would be short, there was a lot that I needed to accomplish in a very limited amount of time. I wouldn't have the luxury of long, drawn-out periods where my challenges could evolve more organically. Me and Mom hit the ground running.

The Truth of Lessons

"Anything that annoys you is teaching patience.
Anyone who abandons you is teaching you how to stand on your own two feet.
Anything that angers you is teaching forgiveness
and compassion.
Anything that has power over you is teaching you
how to take that power back.
Anything you hate is teaching you unconditional love.
Anything you fear is teaching you courage to overcome
your fear.
Anything you can't control is teaching you how to let go."

—Unknown

My Journey to Understand

As I delve into my reading, the topic of lessons jumps to the head of the line and seems to cover a myriad of situations, attitudes, and beliefs. My earliest introduction to lessons occurred in childhood. If you asked me then what I thought of lessons, I probably would have delivered a child's explanation of crime and punishment, hard work, no play, and something unpleasant that takes up a lot of time.

Actually, until the time when I come across a more adult view of the meaning of lessons, I would probably still provide a similar definition. Surprisingly, I learn that there is great meaning and purpose behind our ability to "learn our lessons" in this life. Much of the source material comes from the accounts of Brian Weiss and Dawson Church, who, with their clients, explored past-life lessons, left unresolved, which manifested in physical illness in the current life.

It is a current physical illness that brings these patients to their doctors. As they explore past lives, the therapists discover a direct link between what may have occurred hundreds of years ago and current suffering. For example, one story tells of a man who had been plagued with lifetime migraine headaches. These were debilitating. The headaches occurred in three different areas of his head. Through past-life regression, the patient brought himself to three lives where he had been killed in battle, all by head injuries. After each regression, the therapist asked, "What was the lesson from this life?" Under hypnosis, the answers always come! Our subconscious knows all. Recalling lessons is easy and stress-free in a past-life regression. Once a lesson is learned, there is no reason to suffer anymore. After the sessions were over, the patient became permanently free of his migraines.

If a patient couldn't find the link between a past life and current suffering, the therapist would take them to that area we term LBL, where the exalted wisdom of their guides and angels and other ascended masters could provide insight. This is when I fully discover that the lessons we have chosen to learn in this life are, in fact, great gifts. However it is that we learn our lessons, the important point to remember is, in the spiritual world, all suffering is removed when we understand the lesson! [1]

We are not here to die. We are here to heal! Lessons are about putting things in balance. The Universe is pure energy, and energy that is too much or too little will require an adjustment of some sort so that balance is achieved.

Lessons should be considered gifts then, an opportunity to make things whole again. How do we know that we are faced with an important lesson in this life? A good clue is when we find ourselves engaged with some level of suffering. When we find ourselves unhappy, dissatisfied, or physically ill, among other signs, we are in a state of disease. Something has gone wrong in our lives, and we are not sure of the circumstances behind how this state has been created. But we notice it! If this is the time when we finally decide to do something about our situation, we have just given ourselves another opportunity to live again. Lessons are gifts . . . they buy us the time we need to readjust our trajectory!

Lessons and Time

Interestingly enough, the metaphysical concept of lessons and when they are learned has little relationship to our concept of time. This was presented to me from a dream I had over thirty years ago but didn't understand. When we recently moved to a different part of the country last year, I found my notes on the dream. I believe this was a synchronistic event that presented itself at a time when I was finally ready to understand. At the same time, I was struggling with some of the new concepts from the quantum science arena that revealed the concept of time, as we know it in the earthly realm, is not at all like any other place in the universe. In those dimensions, the past, present, and future exist simultaneously . . . they are stacked. [2] It is only on earth that time is measured with a beginning, a middle, and an end. This means we have only so much time to get the job done. In the Divine, there is no time (as we know it). This means that there is plenty of time to get things done, including clearing up old lessons. If we can eliminate the constraints of time, as our consciousness knows it, we can have instant access to the wisdom of the past and the future for as long as we need it. This provides so much more information! Below is the dream vision I had that shows how our lessons are connected to time. This concept gave me a much greater appreciation of the challenge of lessons that we are here to learn. I was also comforted to know that anything I have to do will not be affected by the stress of time. I will have an eternity to do what I have to do!

> **I am walking on a path in some beautiful woods. I notice someone coming toward me from the direction of the trees. He looks like a wise man with a long beard and a monk-like robe. I slow down as he approaches. I am not afraid. I notice he is carrying a small pouch. As he nears, he opens the pouch and tells me he has some gifts for me. He empties the pouch in my hand. There are three beautiful pearls. He then says to me,**

> **"Because I am a Teacher, I will give you a lesson in Time."**

I knew this was an important dream, which is probably why I saved it. But I didn't understand it . . . especially the quote. What was this business of lessons and what does time have to do with anything? When I was delving into Brian Weiss's work from *Many Lives, Many Masters*, I came across the following:

> **"Time is not as we see time, but rather in lessons learned."**

The answer to my dream mystery! From this, I learn earth's version of time, which is unique only to us, now more closely matches the universal concept of time. We incarnate many, many times on this earth. These incarnations can go back millennia. Incarnation offers us opportunities over and over again to learn the lessons that will bring us closer to Source. Linear time as we know it would not be enough to satisfy all that we need to know, learn, and do. By measuring our lives by lessons learned rather than linear time, we can smooth over the discrepancies of the universal version of time and the earthly one. This means we have all the time in the universe to get the job done!

Patrick's Journal

The Early Years: Daycare provided the very first environment where my second earthly challenge was presented: making friends. Allow me to put this in a different way. Mom was concerned I wouldn't make friends mainly because that was *her* challenge as a military brat. Slowly, but surely, she evaluated every daycare event within the context of how many friends I had. Over time, I not only had difficulties making friends, I had difficulty with "management." My expulsion from three daycares (out of five) over four years set the foundation for my life's theme.

There were positive moments in my daycare experience. Two of the five I attended were awesome. My third daycare was the best. This was a gentle, quiet place with providers that truly loved their little charges and were loaded with an abundance of compassion. It was here I learned a new kind of love. This place provided a wonderful calm that eased me, quieted me, and allowed me to feel safe and secure. The experience lasted about three wonderful months until they went belly up and closed their doors.

Those early years in daycare shook my newly forming personality to the core. I always felt out of place wherever I landed and never seemed to fit in. I would do just about anything to get attention or to get people to look like they liked me. Because I was just a kid, there was only one way to do this. Be disruptive. Taking on an elemental version of the class clown, I can remember getting into fights, breaking things, acting out in a silly way in class . . . generally just pushing everyone's buttons. While most of the kids thought I was funny or cool, the teachers didn't. It didn't matter. By being singled out to be yelled at or put on quiet time, I became the center of attention for that second, and it was good.

My Journey to Understand

I didn't get too far along in my son's story when I was stopped dead in my tracks. Until high school, the daycare years were probably four of the most unhappy years of my life with Patrick. Why wasn't he thriving? I knew so many other young moms with kids in daycare who were doing just fine . . . why not mine?

As I reflected on this time, I remember how desperately I wanted him to have friends. This concern, I discovered later, came about as the result of two things: 1) guilt and 2) a prior limiting belief about myself and *my* childhood that adversely affected Patrick.

Let's deal first with the guilt. When Patrick was born, I took a six-week maternity leave, thinking that would be plenty of time to bond. Even so, I was anxious to get back to work. I had convinced my younger sister to give up a lucrative summer job and instead be my babysitter for six weeks until I could find a proper daycare. Out of the huge reservoir of love she had dwelling in her heart, she agreed.

We had been kicking along rather nicely for a couple of weeks. Things were going well. I entered our condominium complex from the garage one evening and rang the bell to the apartment so my sister could let me in when I got off the elevator. As I was walking down the long hallway to my unit, Julie popped out of the door with baby in arms. I shouted out a joyous greeting, and from quite a distance away, I saw this tiny baby stiffen his body and turn fully sideways. She almost lost him! He was straining so very hard to find the source of that voice he had grown so used to for nine months! I was stunned.

First, I didn't know any infant had the strength to move like that! Second, I was shocked that the act was in response to the sound of my voice. The experience quite took me by surprise. If this child had a thought in his head, I could plainly see it. He knows me. He misses me! He's wondering where I have been. Those were my thoughts. The first niggling of guilt started to gnaw. A communication was stirring. I was amazed and distressed at the same time.

The Journal

Mom talked constantly about my behavior in daycare. She talked about how important it was to have friends. I did have friends, but she didn't know it. Her only contact with the daycare experience was through the teachers who constantly reported on my misdeeds. I liked my friends, but I didn't like the rules. I had no attachment to the teachers so dismissed them and their silly rules. I was lonely.

My Journey to Understand: Enabling Behavior

To understand the dilemma Patrick and I found ourselves in, I had to take a step back and reflect on a later time when Patrick had to go to drug rehab in high school. This particular program involved the entire family. I remember the sessions my husband and I had with Patrick's therapist, and I remember how upset I was to learn that I should attend Ala-non meetings.

Ala-non is an off-shoot of Alcoholics Anonymous for enablers of alcoholics who may have unknowingly participated in the development of another's drug or drinking addiction. I vehemently disavowed this title!

First off, I believed I knew many enablers. I found most of them to be quiet, sensitive "do-gooders" who didn't have the "heart" to cause pain by making tough decisions. I had no problems with making decisions. I made them for everybody! If anything, I was a controller.

Truly, the wishy-washy-ness of enablers was kind of insulting. Clearly, I didn't understand the definition of an enabler. Bottom line, it is this. You are an enabler if you believe that your subject is unable to make decisions on their own, so you do it for them. That's it. Of course, this distinction is fuzzy when dealing with young children because they are truly unable for a time to make solid decisions. It is easy to cross the line between being a nurturing parent and a true enabler.

I had decided that Patrick's problem was that he couldn't make friends. This assuaged my guilt that the *real* problem was my return to work. Some kids just do *not* thrive in daycare. My son was one. Had I stopped at the time to really think about this, I might have made a completely different choice for my son's early life, one that might have resulted in a different outcome.

Later on, as a result of my readings, I discovered another disturbing fact that probably contributed to this odd focus on making friends, and this falls into the area of "limiting beliefs." Mentioned previously, my early life was rather insecure. Because my father was in the Air Force, we moved a lot. He was also gone for months at a time on some missions. There were three of us children at the time, and my mother was very young. It was also the 1950s, where children were to be seen and not heard. My early insecurity was great indeed, and I found solace in having playmates . . . friends. I was on a constant quest and determined that if I didn't have my friends, I was nothing.

I devote an entire section in another chapter to "limiting beliefs" and how we can harbor these thoughts for decades. They are damaging and destructive over time. Often, overcoming false beliefs about ourselves becomes the focus as we work to heal the suffering they inflict. In my personal situation, I experienced much criticism as a child. This is a dangerous thing to experience at such an early age. For me, it resulted in my concluding that I was simply an unlovable child. My belief that I was unlovable led me to friendships where I didn't feel that way. To seal the deal, I unknowingly installed my personal limiting belief about friendships onto Patrick's psyche. Had I known the hold it would take over the next fifteen years, I would have made completely a different choice. Witness the beginnings of "karma-clearing" taking place in this scenario. If our lives had played out differently in this life, I may have been faced with this "friends" issue in some other future lifetime.

Sadly, with this new awareness, I finally recognized my enabling behavior and how my son suffered for it.

The Journal

Throughout my daycare years, I had no sense of purpose. Even children have this sense! Underneath it all, I was angry. Angry that Mom wasn't home, angry I had to go to daycare. The effect at age three was self-destructive behavior and acting out. While I didn't really know the difference, I had no love for myself and felt quite alone. These feelings underscored another developing theme that would continue to play out in various ways for a good part of the rest of my life.

Despite her stubbornness and contrariness, Mom is a realist. She reasoned that just because she felt she was doing the right thing didn't mean she was. I would be going into kindergarten in a few months, and we weren't off to a good start. She was also pregnant with my sister. I was very excited to have a sibling!

She and Dad made the decision for Mom to stay home.

Her decision to quit work resulted in one very, very good thing. I finally made a friend, a best friend, and his name was Edward. He lived across the street from us, and because I was now home during the day, we got to play all day long. Edward was my first lifeline to normal. He was part of a large, extended Filipino family; there were tons of kids, grandparents, aunts, and uncles around to watch us and Edward's younger brothers and cousins. Edward and I had free rein to do what we wanted. In other words, we were indulged.

The contrast between the rules of daycare and the indulgence of playing with Edward were confusing. I was allowed to be "me" with Edward and challenged to be "someone else" when I was in daycare. Of course, I liked the Pat/Edward combo the best. We were as old as we had fingers on one hand, so when we played, we were pretty selfish and self-absorbed. We broke rules, stretched them, and occasionally lied to get what we wanted.

I bring up the lying because I noticed, at the time, that it gave me quite a rush. At first I lied about little things . . . just for the heck of it. As time went by, little lies morphed into more sophisticated lies that generally saved my butt from getting into trouble. It became a game, an addiction of sorts. How much could I get away with? The challenge was to see how far I could take this.

The lying I created all by myself. As lessons go, this will prove to be a fun one to get myself out of when the time comes. It would later prove to be, along with the subject of friends, one of the karmic life lessons I had chosen to address once and for all in this life.

My Journey to Understand

The daycare battle was finally reaching a head. Patrick's behavior was becoming increasingly erratic and needy. The daycare teachers started to call me in for meetings. Everyone thought he had a behavioral problem. Yes, behavior was an issue, but I believe that was likely a byproduct of emotional neglect. He had an emotional problem! The caregivers of the daycares Patrick attended told me he had "psychological" problems. One even went so far as to call him "evil." That did it! It would take a lot of convincing for me to believe that any three-year-old has enough presence of mind to mindfully produce an evil act. It was recommended I take him to a child psychologist.

I am sure psychological problems are possible at this age, but there was nothing physically or mentally wrong with my son nor had there been any sort of severe trauma suffered. Even if his problems were "only" emotional, they were still very debilitating. Understanding, kindness, and some introduction to behavioral strategies could have helped repair these maladies.

I gave the child psychiatrist a try for about six months. We heard nothing except that he is "such a delightful child." I was so confused. And then I realized, *"Of course he is delightful. All they do is play games with him."* He was getting more individual attention from this one person once a week than he ever did in daycare or at home, since my husband and I were both working at the time. Not knowing what to do, I surrendered completely and told my husband, *"This kid doesn't need a shrink, he needs a mom!"* Within a few months, I quit my job and the career I had been building for fifteen years. I was so surprised that not a day went by where I missed it! I was where I needed to be.

Lessons and Agreements

Somewhere along my journey's path, I make the connection that the agreements we make with members of our soul family prior to incarnation are based on those big, personal lessons we are here to learn. Some lessons are big enough and important enough to call for this kind of assistance. That premonition I had when Patrick was born was sent to me as a reminder of the agreement we made together. It would be through his early death in this life that I would finally open my eyes to the truth of my earthly existence and what I need to do to heal myself. This would be *the* lifetime event that would finally crack open my heart so that I could learn and grow.

Lessons, as mundane a topic we might think them to be, hold a very sacred place in the human plan. Keeping in mind that our spiritual goal is to finally become One with Source, we need to be just as perfect. Lessons help us get there. [3]

To Soften the Heart

Concurrent with learning all about lessons, I am led to Gregg Braden, geologist, scientist, metaphysic, and his books about the importance of the heart. It might help to note that at the same time, I was also exploring meditation. Throughout *all* of my reading, a strong emphasis on meditation is advised because *all* of the answers to our questions, our suffering, our dreams, and our desires *will* come from within ourselves. As children of the Divine, we can potentially hold all that is God and Love. We just forgot how. Meditation helps us find our authentic selves, without the encumbrance of limiting beliefs or low-level emotions.

Coincidentally, then, Gregg Braden's concept of Heart/Brain Coherence dovetailed nicely with what I was trying to do with meditation. Braden asks us to open our minds and look to the heart as a "second brain." The heart could, in fact, be termed a second brain as it already holds at least forty thousand brain neurons. Love resides in the heart. This is also where our subconscious memories are stored. This is where we will find our answers. From Braden's point of view, when the heart and the brain are not communicating, when they are not connecting, we are in dissonance. For wonderful things to happen, the heart and brain must be coherent with each other. Taking a few moments to fill one's heart with love and rest in that place for a little while will smooth any incoherence between the brain and the heart. We need them to be working together. All I can report is that when I do a five minute Heart/Brain loving meditation, I feel wonderful for about six hours . . . plenty of time for any recent trauma to pass. [4] [5]

I really like this approach because meditation, like anything else, is a skill that gets better and better with practice. I had been investigating formal meditation programs when I came across the Heart/Brain Coherence approach. It was easy to put my attention on my heart for only five minutes and allow that feeling to permeate. This is a great meditation "primer" if you haven't had the time to find your practice.

Familiar Guidance

So I was agreeable to the fact that I had lessons to learn in this life. Specifically what those lessons were eluded me. I was a novice in meditation and simply didn't know the questions to ask. What are the lessons I need to learn in this life?

On cue, James Van Praagh, well-known medium and spiritualist and author of *Wisdom From Your Spirit Guides: A Handbook To Contact Your Soul's Greatest Teachers*, categorizes all of the lessons we need to learn into two topics: On Treating Self and On Treating Others. This is familiar. I believe this message is also in the Bible.

How we treat others *directly* mirrors how we feel about ourselves. I had to keep reading this to understand the simple message. We are all of Source. We are the same . . . to the extent a mirror is a reflection of ourselves, we are a reflection of others. This is a big lesson because it requires us to know ourselves far more than we do now. This is the way to understand others . . . by understanding ourselves. We are all connected. To this end, Van Praagh offers three cardinal rules to get us on the path:

"Never judge another. Let yourself Love. Learn to Forgive."

Van Praagh also cautions us to never relinquish our power. Never be less than who you are. To give oneself up in order to maintain a relationship that may have already been lost, for example, is relinquishing power altogether. So much of the time we have so little faith in ourselves, we give our power away. Sometimes this is easier to do than being true to oneself.

"Happiness is an inside job. Don't assign anyone else that much power over your life."

—Mandy Hale

The last "lesson" offered under Treating Others is to "give without expectation." This one says it all. When dealing with others, keep the scoreboard off the table. Practice the habit of giving freely.

The concepts above are a great place to start meditation if you're like me and just had no clue. Really thinking about what these suggestions mean and where the holes are in my own life that I need to fill is a beginning. As I continue with my practice, I note my approach changes and shifts every time I learn something new or finally understand what I need to know. It's a constant work in progress.

Self-Love

The second message Van Praagh delivers has to do with how we treat ourselves. This is the area of my greatest challenge. How have I done with my ability to love myself? In the beginning, not so very well. As revealed in Patrick's journal, my concern with his making friends had to do with my personal insecurity in this area. I started young with the idea that I was unlovable, then nurtured that belief for the next two decades until I completely forgot it was a problem. Bottom line, the message is this.

> **One has to be in love with oneself before any kind of quality love can be delivered to others. If we can see the love for ourselves, we'll see it in others. This is how the mirror works.**

Over the course of this soul journey, despite my drive to get answers to my questions, I realized my true quest had to do with finding unconditional self-love. Without this love, I was going nowhere. I would have to start at the beginning. Forgiveness of self was the way to start. Forgiveness of others comes later.

Today, I certainly don't have all the answers regarding the entirety of the lesson(s) I need to learn, but I can tell you this: all of it changed me, and this is what I did learn.

Compassion

Telling my son's story opened my eyes to how mightily he struggled with his challenges. Patrick was a quiet, reserved person. He loved to talk but chose his words carefully. Because I wasn't much of a listener, I misunderstood his quietness as disrespect and dismissiveness. While not outwardly displayed, I had no idea how insecure he was about fitting in. Further, I was confused at times because he seemed to be shutting others out, which maybe implied he didn't care.

I got so much wrong.

Compassion was a skill I lost in childhood. Viewed as a weakness, if you showed compassion, you were ripe for an attack. You were vulnerable and therefore beatable. To muster up empathy was not in my repertoire.

When I use Patrick's words to tell his story, I can feel the energy he devoted to learning, hearing, and doing things that were very difficult to do. I relate to his frustrations as well as his joys and victories. I was such a task master. *Let's just get this done and move on.* I had forgotten how to feel compassion. Shedding tears in awe and inspiration over his struggle as well as remorse for misinterpreting his intentions during his life was the first clue that my heart had finally been pierced. From this wound, I know I will heal.

Forgiveness

I was hard on Patrick in those early years. I was so afraid he wouldn't have friends. That, I think, was an early smokescreen for the guilt I felt returning to work, but my own issues with friendship provided an opportunity to create a problem for my son and take my mind off my guilt. So I became the Great Enabler. When I learned this, it made me sad. I never meant to add a problem to his life, but the damage was done. The only way to move forward was to forgive myself once and for all. I don't think I had ever before forgiven myself for anything. I was very good at defending all of my actions, but self-forgiveness was never considered.

Loving Self

This has been and continues to be one of the hardest lessons for me. By the time I was thirty-five, I was really only proud of two things: having a successful career and becoming a mother. But these were just "things." These were trophies that showed the world that I was competent and able and normal, but they didn't really make me like me.

When I started my "personal rehab" decade in my early forties, the issue at the heart of my desire to do this was the relationship with my own mother. It was such a distressing time for me because I knew in my heart that there was nothing that could change her. I knew I would never get anything "motherly" from her, but the situation had to be resolved. This was difficult, but I wrote about it in my journal for months. I also added one more condition to my recovery . . . *I decided not to blame anyone for my state of being.* There was a part of me that intuitively knew that I had to "show up" and participate in this particular mother/daughter relationship for it to manifest as it did. Therefore, I could not consider myself a victim. The retrieval of my happiness, then, would be a solo gig. I took complete control over how I would do this.

So I followed those things that I knew would make me happy. I indulged my passion for the arts both as an admirer and a participant. I didn't talk myself out of doing anything I wanted to do, even if I thought people would laugh at me (acting). My determination was fierce, and I was committed until something changed.

And change it did! It took ten years, but I was a new woman in just about every way. This is one of my proudest accomplishments. I did it without the benefit of all this wonderful knowledge I am learning today. I did it without the benefit of the medical field. I did it without a support group or cheerleading section. I just did it.

This was the first great act of love I did for myself.

Today I know so much more, and I know I still need to work on self-love. With the help of meditation, workshops, reading, and a good support group of like-minded individuals, I work every day on loving myself. This is higher-level work, and the effects have been profound for me. It isn't nearly as hard today as it was twenty years ago.

Because I feel myself differently, I notice I am attracting different people, situations, and benefits in a different way. It's a fascinating experience and one I am not likely to change. This is the way I work now. Had I not taken care of the more "basic" improvements in the years before Patrick died, I would not have been ready to do what I am doing today. Some part of that Agreement we made so long ago is becoming clearer.

In time, I eventually forgave my mother. It was long after my rehab period and at least ten years after Patrick's death. But when I did finally forgive her, I felt reborn! I had, by this time, genuinely learned that I was not unlovable. I had found many, many lovable aspects to my nature. By erasing the self-erected barriers to self-love, I had forgiven myself in the process. It was a piece of cake to forgive my mom!

CHAPTER FOUR

The Truth of Energy

Heavenly Hindsight

WHEN I FIRST PASSED from the earthly realm to the heavens, I experienced an explosion of light and a burst of expansion. I was not aware that my body wasn't with me because I felt just like my old self. My personal consciousness was taking in an incredible display of geometric shapes of all sizes and colors. It was a veritable kaleidoscope of shifting angles, circles, squares, spirals, and colors in constant movement, never repeating anything that previously occurred. Further, I felt so expansive, so large. I was everywhere at once. It was then I realized I was not incarnate anymore. I was spirit.

It was just so beautiful. I wasn't afraid at all . . . just amazed and curious. I was still a bit unclear as to where I was, but I could stay here and explore forever. And then it came . . . inside my essence an implosion of pure love bubbled from me to the surface and joined with a massive, powerful love, the likes I have never before experienced. The effect was similar to an enormous electrical shock which wasn't painful at all. Rather, it was saturated with ecstasy.

This was God! It was undeniable.

And when I connected with God, I found I was connected to everything that had ever hosted life, been life, or is life. I understood why I was here. I understood the secrets of the universe. I knew where I had been and why, and I knew where I was going. Bliss is too common of a word to describe the experience, but it's the best our good earth could come up with. I felt so large and so small at the same time.

For the longest time, the topic of energy on earth has been misunderstood. Humans are so wrapped up in their three-dimensional world, feeling separate from others because of the bodies they find themselves in, that many of them can't see beyond their noses. It's an insular world governed by experiences to the body, both pleasant and not, and from which they learn to define themselves.

The linear nature of time in this dimension further confuses things because it puts attention on endings and, frankly, makes us feel rushed. There is only so much time to get this, go there, do this, and be here. What we do can feel incredibly insignificant because our belief is when our time runs out, our dreams and everything else can run out as well.

After my arrival here, I learned pretty quickly that our beautiful planet is in severe jeopardy. This particular war and conflict phase, which is nearing its five-thousand-year end, has been especially harsh. The number of people on the planet and the rapid advance of technology have been instrumental in harming our world, so much so that, in his infinite wisdom, Source has agreed to let those of us who reside here do what we can to help our humans.

If the planet's inhabitants continue on their current course, it is likely earth could be destroyed. It's actually more likely that the planet will somehow survive, but life for the few that remain will be nothing like it is today. This could be construed as a good thing by many, but Source loves *all* of us . . . yes, *all* of us . . . and he wants us to survive. So we are getting help from those like me from the other side so that those earth's inhabitants who are ready to receive this information will have the knowledge and wisdom needed to get the word out and help do something about it.

As an incarnate being living on earth, I did not know that my time would be so short. I just felt driven. I often felt anxious and as if I was "out of time." As a spiritual being, I knew what my job was and that I had plenty of time to get it all done, but the earthly effect created a high state of agitation most of the time. I had such large plans. One would think it's unfair to take someone so young, but we are only here as long as we have purpose.

I lived a full life. I was able to express myself and contribute to humanity with the gifts I was given. I was presented with lessons that I needed to learn. I was able to inspire others to learn. Not bad for eighteen tiny years of life!

The theme of my earthly life was established in my earliest years. It wasn't a complicated one, but it certainly begat some serious damage. Mom, in her desperation to give me a different childhood than she had, impressed upon me that the number and quality of friends I had would be *the* most important thing. It was to this end that I was directed. By the time I was almost six, the intention had been set and gelled. The ultimate outcome, however, was less than ideal. How I dealt with it was to be a major earthly challenge.

The Truth of Energy

Energy and how we understand it is one of the most important truths revealed. It had been a mystery until some of its secrets were uncovered in Einstein's equation. From this, we have discovered that each of us has the ability to manipulate and redirect energy toward a different outcome. We can create new matter with just our minds. All of God's children can do this.

My Journey to Understand

As I was intuitively jumping from one topic to another during my learning phase, I was surprised to find myself at the front door of science. Never a science fan in school, I had no previous interest in ever exploring, until the metaphysical led me there. My first stop is quantum physics, and the star headliner is energy.

Despite my lifelong love of the metaphysical, I am a structured, rational person. At first, I found all of this information on past lives, in between lives, agreements, spirit guides, angels, and soul groups, etc., pretty heady stuff. At a gut level, however, it felt authentic. It resonated. It always has. Yet I yearned for proof. I was tired of trading one set of beliefs based on faith (my religion) for another set (metaphysical), also based on faith. When I studied this material thirty years ago, there was no scientific proof that any of what I wanted to believe existed. As I jumped back on my path of discovery for a second time, I had huge surprises waiting.

I discovered that energy and how we understand it was one of the most important truths *and* source of power revealed to me. It was the one thing that helped me understand how the universe worked. It was a thing that I learned I could manipulate any way I want. It was something that I learned I could use to bring great happiness and fulfillment to my life. How was this possible? What was energy?

What is Energy?

It was only as recent as the early twentieth century that the true nature of energy was revealed in a dramatic equation, $E=MC^2$. Simply stated, all matter is energy, even though some matter is so dense, you can't imagine it in its energy form. From this point, our knowledge of energy has grown exponentially. Today, as more people learn of the power of energy, they have also come to know that they can also alter the seemingly rigid path of destruction most humans find themselves travelling. This is when they discover that they have the ability to manipulate and redirect energy into specific outcomes. This is a gift we possessed eons ago and which we used regularly but threw away with the advent of tools, technology, and communities where labor was organized.

What is this magic and how is it so easy for us to direct? The equation itself states the obvious. *Everything* is energy. Even solid matter is pure energy at its most dense. Years ago, when I was studying Edgar Cayce, he made a statement that "thoughts are things." When I read this for the first time, I could not imagine what he was talking about. I couldn't imagine a thought becoming some form of matter.

Today, I know that thoughts, words, feelings, emotions, and everything in between is energy. Since energy changes matter, we can eventually expect to see "form" created from these energetic sources. I attribute most of what I have learned on the subject to Dr. Joe Dispenza from his books *Becoming Supernatural*, *You Are the Placebo*, and *Evolve Your Brain*, and Dawson Church's *Mind to Matter: The Astonishing Science of How Your Brain Creates Material Reality*. Further, Dispenza's workshops are practically science labs where participant brain wave patterns are measured during meditation. Why is it important to know that the thoughts we think are pure energy? Because quantum science has proven that all energy can change matter. There is no useless energy in the quantum field. It exists until it is called upon to do something.

"Yet only one thing must be remembered: there is no effect without a cause and there is no lawlessness in creation."

—Rumi

Along with the words of Rumi, the world of quantum science also brings us to the knowledge that there is no chaos in the universe. Everything is ordered and logical. Everything is part of a plan or a purpose. Despite outward appearances, there is no randomness in the universe that God created. Just because energy can't always be seen doesn't mean it doesn't exist. Why should we be bothered with this at all? By truly understanding, we can teach ourselves how to use this gift to bring great transformation to our lives.

"If you wish to find the secrets of the Universe, think in terms of Energy, Frequency, and Vibration."

—Nikola Tesla

Energy is characterized by frequency and vibration. Vibrations refer to the oscillating movement of atoms and particles caused by energy. Frequency, measured in Hertz units (Hz), is the *rate* at which vibrations and oscillations occur. Frequencies are also used to discern and differentiate vibrational patterns [1]. We already know, through our familiarity with radio wave frequencies, that frequencies carry information. To get the information we want, we just have to "tune in" to the right channel. It is the same with the rest of the energy frequencies in the Universe. Which ones do we want to tune in to, and how do we do it?

One of our biggest challenges here on this earth is our ability to manage our emotions. Emotions are a very big deal. They are also pure energy. I don't think anyone reading this believes that we can't *feel* the effect of an angry outburst directed toward us. We aren't dealing with matter here, but an energetic effect that is just loaded with information. As that angry outburst is hurled our way, we likely understand the message before any words have been uttered. Anger is a great example of what energy can do . . . we have all been involved.

Part of the problem of dealing with emotional energy on earth is the 3D body we are challenged to live in for the duration of this and all other lives. We can feel so separate and so alone. We don't have that direct connection to another's soul because we need to filter everything through our bodies. We are charged to *feel*, but the bodily mechanism through which that happens is cumbersome. The human process dictates that we can only feel energy by looking for clues in our physical bodies. It is the energy that a particular emotion produces that paves the path to meaning. It is important, then, that we learn to pay attention to our emotions. We need our bodies to physically experience the events that come into our lives. [2]

It is the events and experiences we have throughout our lives, along with our reactionary, emotional state while dealing with them, that influence the *beliefs* we create for and about ourselves. Some of these beliefs may be grand and wonderful. There are those who have somehow managed to exist here with a wonderful personal belief system intact. These are the ones we notice who also have extremely blessed lives. Most of us, however, have somehow attached limited (negative) personal beliefs to experiences that can contribute nothing but additional challenge and suffering. These beliefs are the ones that hold us back. [3]

The last scientific point on energy at this time has to do with the infinite number and types of frequencies and vibrations of energy. Dr. Joe Dispenza spends much time on this, for its understanding is the key to the magic of transformation. All frequency of energy in the universe carries the information of a possibility. We view unactualized frequencies as possibilities. When we put our attention on these frequencies, they instantly turn into probabilities. All frequencies are attracted to other frequencies that have the same or similar vibration.

Assuming we accept this premise, how do we bring wonderful and benevolent probability to our lives? We do it through our emotions! The Universal Law of Attraction (aka Like Attracts Like) is now called into play. Usually accomplished through deep contemplation, writing, or meditation, we can create high brain wave frequencies through an elevated emotion that attracts similar frequencies from the universal arena. In order to be helped, we must be heard! There is more on this idea of manifestation to come, but by recognizing emotion as a powerful catalyst, we are on our way!

Using our emotions to attract specific energy frequencies to us is foundational for changing energy into matter. This is what manifestation is all about. In Patrick's story, we can see the stirrings of manifestation. Still a child, he was trying to figure things out. Children can manifest so much easier than adults. They haven't yet learned, through cultural conditioning, that they can't always have or be what they want. Our early lives instead, are manifestation magic. [4]

The Journal: Elementary and Middle School

I was finally going to a real school! Five miserable years in daycare had taken its toll. Mom, by this time, had quit work to stay at home, and I got a new sister in the bargain. Because she was home all day, I got to play outside in our neighborhood and in doing so met my first best friend, Edward.

When I started kindergarten at the local public school, I made a couple of friends, but they weren't Edward. Not having much in the way of social skills, I likely came on a bit aggressively. I got into some scrapes on the playground and made a number of visits to the principal's office. On the positive side, I was introduced to performing in school plays, several different sports (soccer, T-ball, and baseball) and computers!

My absolute favorite class was computers! Computer class was held once a week in the library. In kindergarten, we actually learned to write using computers. Now *this* was home! I didn't know it at the time, but my work with computers would become a true passion in the years to come and my skill in using them would play significantly in my final contributions to life on earth.

Problems, however, with my behavior still persisted. By the time I completed the first half of third grade, I found out we were moving! Our house, having been on the market for ten months, finally sold just before Christmas that year. We temporarily moved to Saratoga, about an hour away, and lived in my dad's parents' home there until we found a new place to live.

This meant I had to transfer to yet another school in the middle of a year. My time at the new school actually went really well, but not for the right reasons. I was terrified. Terrified at having to move to a new place, at having to make new friends, and I missed Edward tremendously. I was in such a state of shock that I didn't have the energy to bring out my misbehaving ways, so I stayed quiet . . . quiet, but alone.

In six months' time, we moved again to our new home. It was closer to Edward and where most of my mom's family lived. We joined a country club, and I would be starting fourth grade at the local parish school at the end of the summer. It was at this time I remember making the decision to change. I wanted a new life. I wanted to fit in!

My Journey to Understand: Attention and Awareness

As I review this little piece of Patrick's life, I realize that I took little to no time to really consider how this move would have affected him. I was so busy with everything else. As a child, I couldn't wait to move. Living the military life afforded me this privilege. Somehow, I just assumed that my children would see things through my eyes, though I would never have this expectation of anyone else.

Patrick's ability at nine years old to create a "new" person to go along with his "new" home is impressive in retrospect. He had a sincere desire to change. He obviously put much energy into these thoughts. I bring it up now because the process he used naturally is the same as what I have recently learned in meditation to bring new opportunity and abundance to my own life.

Attention and Awareness vs. Intention

As we deliberately work to attract new energy to our lives, I learn that *intention* has little value except to start the process or continue it. Don't misunderstand. A strong intention is critical to making life changes and is one of the very first steps. But intention without action is just wasted energy. Many confuse wishing with intentions. For manifestation, intention without action is the same as wishing. Wishing rarely gets us what we want. What is the magic key? It is *attention* to an outcome or a possibility that begins the process that can change our reality. It is the *awareness* we apply to the process and to the desired outcome that results in actual material change. [5]

We are manipulating energy whenever and wherever we are putting our attention. Dawson Church in his book, *Mind to Matter*, states, "One of the things that determine the direction in which a swarm of possibilities (particles) collapses in the act of observation is . . . *where you put your attention, i.e. your energy.*" This is called The Observer Effect. [6]

Scientists discovered, at the particle level, that observation brings "life" (energy) to the particle, but only when observed. If you look away, the particle seems to disappear. It's a complicated science, but at the end of the day, the message is the same. Awareness and attention have the power to influence, change, and materialize energy. By the way, I learned that by putting attention on the possibilities that exist in the universe, we will "collapse" that possibility into a probability. We are changing energy into matter. Now we have something that can be seen as well as imagined.

By putting his attention on becoming a "calmer" person, Patrick was actually focusing his efforts in such a way that that he could condense possibility (energy) into a powerful new force (probability) that generates a new frequency or vibration. This new energy then holds enough power, because of awareness, to attract more of the same. The Law of Attraction at work!

The Journal: Skateboard Parks, Inline Skating, Snowboarding, Drugs

I just wanted a calmer life. Maybe now, with the new school, new house, new neighborhood, and the opportunities at the country club, that would happen.

And it did! I did well in fourth and fifth grades, both academically and socially. I still missed Edward, though, and I was still unhappy. I was drifting.

And so, whenever Mom sensed these shifts, she decided a new school was in order. Rather than allow me to continue through to the eighth grade, she enrolled me in the public middle school. She reasoned it was here I would make the friends I would ultimately have in high school so wanted me to have a head start on the process.

The school I attended was *huge*. I was assigned to one of three sixth-grade classrooms. I didn't know a soul. Now, when I'm in a new situation, I keep pretty quiet and to myself. Over the years, however, I found that being funny and creating little disturbances in the back of the room, usually making fun of someone who did something kind of dumb, was a good ice-breaker. The kids in my "performance" area were always cracking up.

My teacher actually liked me despite all this. She decided I was a leader type so assigned me several positions of responsibility inside the classroom. This definitely kept me occupied. I had a great year! I was on the honor roll, and I made a new friend. His name was Matt.

Matt thought I was hysterical, and we carried our antics into the lunchroom and the playground. We were a troublesome duo, but hey! He was my friend. After about a month or so, I officially changed the spelling of my name from Pat to Patt. So, here we were, Matt and Patt!

By seventh grade, Matt and I were assigned different classrooms. We still remained friends, but my world was expanding. We moved around a little more in seventh grade, and I would see Matt from time to time, so we would pick up where we left off when we did cross paths . . . just for old time's sake.

It was also in seventh grade I found another new best friend. Eric was a quiet guy who lived nearby and who would play a big role as my best friend for the rest of middle school and a good part of high school.

Seventh grade was an important year for me in many ways. Using Mom's language of energy, it was the first year when the effects of everything that came before started to manifest into a rough cut of the personality I would wear for most of the rest of this particular earthly life. For me, it was the "Best of Times and the Worst of Times."

I was eleven, nearly twelve, when I discovered inline skating. I had been watching X Games and ESPN2 at the time and was majorly impressed with inline skating. Edward and I did manage to get together for some play dates, and after nagging our moms for weeks, we finally had our first pair of inline skates. Skateboard parks were being built everywhere, but until our local park was done, we practiced our grinds, airs, cess-slides, and toe/heel maneuvers on any illegal sidewalk or staircase with rail we could find. It was a heady time! My athleticism was morphing into something concrete.

My fascination with computers continued unabated since kindergarten. We had one computer in the house in those days, and it was downstairs where the guest room and second family room were located. It was here that I discovered the online game of *Dungeons and Dragons* and jumped in.

The attraction to computers is pretty easy to trace. It runs in the family. My grandpa on Dad's side was a research physicist at IBM working on new digital software that could track weather patterns from space. My aunt, Dad's sister, received her doctorate in computer science at UCLA and also worked at IBM designing computer hardware. My grandma was a math teacher, and my cousin received her doctorate degree in theoretical mathematics at MIT. My dad was his high school class valedictorian, and after a technology-laden career at a major bank, he founded a digital media business. Computers came easy for me.

Computer game playing was nothing like it is today. I played *Dungeon and Dragons* online, in real time, against real players, using nothing but code. I loved this! It's like speaking another language but with a keyboard. I loved the logic of code and really discovered myself in this activity. Computers would be my life!

I would also come to find out that my obsession with this game and the code that came with it resulted in an addiction of sorts. Later on in high school when things got pretty gnarly, Mom called me out and announced that this game playing was just a "gateway drug." It turned out she was right.

On the plus side, I discovered novels and an aptitude for writing. My favorite author at the time was Ken Follett. He wrote a lot of novels and always introduced the new technology of the times he was writing about. My seventh-grade teachers were impressed with my choice of authors. They told Mom that my reading interests were way above seventh grade. Whatever. I just liked the stories.

During this lucid period in my life, I discovered so many things that not only fascinated me, but that I was also good at. Computers, coding, reading, writing, public speaking, opinionating (thanks, Mom!), nature, and more were a few of my regularly scheduled activities. As middle school progressed, I found my friends through these common interests.

My Journey to Understand Manifestation

To understand how Patrick changed so dramatically during his middle and early high school years, I really had to drill down on this energy business. It seemed that in my search for answers, I had to become my own experiment. Most of my work in this area was through exploring various forms of meditation. I had a rudimentary understanding, at the time, that I could attract new possibilities to my life by putting attention to a specific outcome. I understood if I attached an elevated emotion to the outcome and could sustain those feelings of enthusiasm and joy, I could manifest just about anything I wanted. Truly, for me, this was a miracle. I had no idea any of us were capable of this power.

This did take some time. In the beginning, I was listening to guided meditations that just helped me to relax. I never considered myself a real candidate for meditation. I was just too hyper. I have never been able to take a nap, much less even consider fifteen minutes of meditation. I was so surprised at how easy it came to me the first time. I did my fifteen minutes and never felt better. I reasoned, at the time, there was always fifteen minutes in a day where this could be done. It seemed a good investment.

After a time, I started researching more about meditation to understand what I was really supposed to be doing other than relaxing. When I got to Dr. Dispenza's scientific approach, I learned how to purposefully direct my meditations toward specific outcomes. This proved to be a big commitment, but it was so exciting! Like anything, practice makes perfect, but this was a commitment I was making for myself. This was for me. I would benefit. I made the choice to practice every day.

In time, I found myself "becoming." Writing is always something I have loved to do. Many of my earlier Joe Dispenza meditations focused on the possibility of being a writer. I put much attention to how I imagined a writer's life to be. I imagined the joy I would feel with my first published book. I imagined new activities associated with my new profession. I had to imagine a lot! All of my thoughts were positive and elevated. I brought the joy of my future life to my present one. I worked on this for months.

And so it was with Patrick during that magical time when he found himself for a little while. He had made some significant changes in his personality and demeanor. Inspired by his friendship with Edward, Patrick envisioned himself as a skateboarding athlete. His joy and anticipation about anything having to do with this activity was pervasive. How did he do that? He was attracted to the sport; he studied it incessantly by watching TV shows and local athletes at the park. He began to talk the talk and walk the walk. He practiced constantly, and his outings with Edward were the opportunity to show off all his hard work and his athletic prowess.

Why is any of this important? Both my approach and that of my son created a scenario for manifestation in areas where neither of us had experience, yet both of us *believed* we could transform. Both of us had to believe we could create a different reality. There is a lot of detail and a lot of imagination at play, but this is authentic manifestation. It does take a lot of work!

> *"Imagination is everything. It's the preview of life's coming attractions."*
>
> **—Albert Einstein**

Learning how to put attention to a possibility and bring it to life with elevated emotions was just one side of the meditation equation. I was purposefully manifesting so that I could transform my entire self. At the time, this was difficult to do because I had yet to learn about those "limiting beliefs" I mentioned earlier. I had to do more than imagine a new life . . . I had to imagine it without any of the emotional chains that had been holding me back for nearly half a century. I had to break the connections once and for all.

While limiting beliefs are usually created in childhood, they aren't set and gelled until we have firmly entrenched them in our psyches. Patrick was young enough to make significant changes to his life without having to deal with eliminating an old belief system that could hold him back. Children just seem to do this naturally. (He was still building his belief system about friends, but it wasn't "set" just yet.)

The Journal

In eighth grade, Mom introduced me to snowboarding. Now, don't get me wrong. Mom does *not* snowboard, but she skis. What she was really doing was creating a weekend diversion for me so I wouldn't get into trouble. Since my studies were still a bit off and always last minute, I had way too much free time on my hands, especially on the weekends.

Snowboarding was way cool! It's just a different version of inline skating. Every Saturday, Dad would drive me to the ski club drop-off place where I would board a bus for a day trip to Squaw Valley or Alpine or any of the other Tahoe resorts.

It was on the bus that I really got to know Eric, who would be my best friend through most of high school. Eric and I met on a field trip in sixth grade and hit it off pretty well. We did school projects together, and he lived nearby, so it was easy to visit. Eric's mom and my mom thought it would be wholesome for us to learn to snowboard. Unbeknownst to any of the moms, however, it was also on the bus that I was seriously introduced to pot and other recreational drugs.

The process was a slow one. Eric was pretty shy, but he was a rebellious dude underneath it all and, like me, took advantage of numerous opportunities that were sure to annoy his parents. I went along for the ride because I liked Eric. He was funny, and he was loyal. We would also be going to the same high school together, so I was set in the friend department. Eric had a couple of other good friends, and they became mine as well. I didn't have a problem experimenting with drugs. I liked the way they made me feel, and they insured friendships for the next four years.

"Oh, what tangled webs we weave . . . " The insecurities of my younger years had a bigger impact on me than I gave them credit for at the time. By the time I had reached middle school, my methods for dealing with my shortcomings had clearly established themselves as habits. In order to boost my self-esteem, I sought to portray a "cooler" me. A little pot, a little booze really helped me to fit in. Because I had been kicked out of so many preschools, I already believed I was different from everyone else. By the time I was in middle school, my coping strategies were evolving. I was becoming addicted to using relationships! I really didn't care about relationships that really mattered, such as family or teachers.

It takes energy to create a physical manifestation of the

thoughts we have. As children we do this naturally. We are born with certain gifts and, if we are lucky enough to recognize them because of opportunity or other means, we tend to put awareness on them. For some, this may be a musical gift or some other area where we demonstrate an early aptitude. We find ourselves attracted to people and activities where we can express ourselves. We experiment and try things out. If these gifts aren't taken out of context by a hovering parent or other caregiver and are allowed to naturally evolve, we can benefit mightily. As children, we do this with our eyes closed. Our energies just flow.

When we are older, the effort is more difficult. Life actually gets in the way sometimes and distracts us from our purpose. We create obstacles and roadblocks because our ability to focus is compromised. There are so many other new things to pay attention to. The choices we make either smooth the road ahead or make it very, very bumpy. However you look at it, it is how we use the energy around us to either continue on our way or change our lives. It's all part of the journey here in this world. I picked the bumpy road.

I was thirteen when the skate park was finished. Mom would drop Edward and me off for a couple of hours and then come pick us up. We got pretty good at tricks, but we had competition and had to share the course. There were guys there that were really awesome. Of course, this just spurred me on to keep up.

By the time I was fourteen, I came to the realization that my body just wasn't cut out for the tumbles, falls, crashes, and more. I never did break anything, but my body was battered. I didn't realize until a few years later that the beating I took at the skate park was partially due to my deteriorating physical condition from the drugs I was experimenting with. At the time, though, I decided I would have to get my jollies just watching X Games. I gave up inline skating.

My Journey to Understand: Limiting Beliefs

To understand how Patrick transformed his sweet, innocent grade school and middle school self into something barely recognizable by high school, I had to really dig deep. This might be a good time to ask why *I* have to dig deep when the situation I am trying to understand has to do with my son's life.

To begin with, other than a smattering of information over the years that I was attracted to, I really didn't know anything about what I was learning. All of it was pretty new to me and much of it, frankly, surprising. I realized that, in learning, I had to shift my perception, open my mind, and just allow it all to settle. After that, I personally tested every claim.

Metaphysics dictates a spiritual practice. Throughout *all* of my reading, there was at least one if not many other references to "the answers are inside of us." What answers? How would I know I had an answer? What would happen? I reasoned, if I could find answers for myself, I would find the answers about my son. I would become the lab. Limiting beliefs, which became my target area, was the first area of opportunity and challenge. This choice also paralleled Patrick's own experience with limiting beliefs as his early experiences with daycare informed him that he really didn't "fit in." In response, he was designing a world of friends based on "using relationships."

Limiting Beliefs

Limiting beliefs define the personal, mostly negative beliefs one has about oneself. Not all of our beliefs are limiting. Some of them are quite wonderful. It's the negative beliefs we have that limit any spiritual growth or progression. Companions to limiting beliefs can include fear, insecurity, self-consciousness, and other low frequency, limiting emotions. How and when do limiting beliefs get installed?

Let's visit thoughts becoming things again. Attention to an outside event or experience will activate a thought. Attention to a thought will also activate a thought. Our response to these events or thoughts will activate energy in the form of an emotion. Our brain picks up the energy (emotion) we are experiencing as a result of the event or thought. The brain then signals the body to produce chemicals and elixirs that match the specific type of energy produced by the emotion. Both our physical and mental selves begin to match our beliefs. Over time, all of these similar thoughts will create a state of being or an "attitude" of how we view ourselves. We now have the package through which everyone else views us. [7]

The manner in which this limiting belief comes into our consciousness may have happened decades earlier. Many of us experience our first limiting beliefs in childhood. An early childhood filled with illness, for example, may create a limiting belief that we are just "sickly" people and need a lot of care. As we hold this belief close to us for the next couple of decades, we may face a lifetime filled with illness and attention. Our beliefs are powerful, and the Law of Attraction is real. We continue to attract the same.

> **Limiting beliefs are the weeds in your garden. They thrive and grow by hiding themselves amongst the blooms. Many are quite clever. Sometimes they look like the real deal. Sometimes they look harmless and like nothing at all. It isn't until some time has passed that the garden isn't vibrant anymore. There are no more blooms . . . just this weed. Now it is obvious, and it's a big problem.**

I needed to prove these teachings for myself. With meditation, I can take the information inside and personally explore and experience. The idea that I was "unlovable" as a child carried well into my adult years. As an adult, I created a more grown-up version of this and considered myself a "difficult personality." In response, I believed I had to work harder than anyone else. I became very good at what I did, but I was also competitive, jealous, and aggressive. Fortunately,

I also had an excellent sense of humor (which I believe I inherited from my dad) and, as a result, was able to push through to my goals with relative success. The stress, however, was taking its toll. I had my first ulcer when I was twenty-six years old. When I meditated, I focused on these feelings of unlovability. Where did I feel it? What was it telling me? In quiet, the answers come. My healing remedy was always a massive dose of unconditional self-love. I delivered this dose to my child self. The work I did lasted for about two months.

There is one other example of the effects of damaging limiting beliefs. From Susan Watkins and her book *Conversations with Seth* [8], the spirit guide, Seth, speaks to a regular group of metaphysics through a medium. The accounts and writings occurred in the late sixties and early seventies. The following paraphrases one compelling session and became the story that helped me clear up my own confusion on the topic.

George was a talented working artist at the time and had been a member of an advanced psychic group for a while. Though he was clearly gifted as an artist, the financial rewards and recognition from his work eluded him. Many people admired his work, but they weren't buying.

When he brought his problem to Seth, George admitted there was only one style of art he created that interested people, and that was his *trompe de l'oeil* work. George considered this art form beneath his ability. This was his first limiting belief. With encouragement from Seth, George revealed a host of additional limiting beliefs he carried regarding his gift.

- *Trompe de l'oeil* work made George feel like a hack. He did not consider this his most creative work.
- George considered the "Establishment" as uncreative. They were "boring" people.
- George considered himself an "artiste" and felt he needed to put distance between himself and the Establishment.

- ◆ George truly believed that art should not be exchanged for money. He didn't think it appropriate.
- ◆ As an artist, he sought to set himself apart and aside from the Establishment for which he had no respect.

Seth's response was eye-opening. He pointed out those masses of humanity that George considered to be uncreative, stupid, and boring somehow *knew* not to buy his more important artwork because they *sensed it really wasn't meant for them.* How is this possible? George's *attitude* about his work permeated his creations! The energy he carried while creating his pieces could not help but be infused into them. I understood this at an elemental level when I often wondered why a meal made by Grandma tasted so much better than one made by someone else. Grandma infused her meals with love!

Seth offered, "Art is meant to be a bridge from one world to another. The Artist speaks to those who can't speak." He advised George to "produce art that will become a spark of recognition to others." When George learned to bring a new *attitude* to *all* of his work that reflected "the joy and vitality of others," others would see themselves in his work. They would buy.

There is a happy end to the story as George did manage to get over himself in due course. He stopped denying himself and others of his gifts to share. His work as an artist eventually became known internationally and provided a decent income.

I imagine this is why they call the effort of "discovering yourself" a journey. It can seem like a long trip to something or somewhere without much of a map. We are all so different. Our perceptions are completely unique, so it's impossible to use one roadmap for all.

**"I was on a journey to find myself,
but the journey found me instead."**

Energy and Healing

While my personal journey focused on emotional and spiritual healing, I could not ignore the implications for good health. I took a slight diversion from my path to study the benefits. Similar to manifesting a new and different life, we can adapt the same process of using highly charged elevated emotions to heal our physical body. Energy is the power behind untold miracles for physical healing. As a matter of fact, miracles are just one product of the day-to-day life of Energy.

Dr. Joe Dispenza, in his book *Becoming Supernatural: How Common People are Doing the Uncommon* [9], applies a spiritual approach to healing through his understanding of science and medicine. By the way, the more we understand the mechanics of what we wish to change, the better the outcome will be. Dr. Dispenza, as a chiropractor, used his personal knowledge of the spine to heal his own severely broken back from a bike accident. Told he would never walk again, he healed himself with his thoughts. Those thoughts helped him visualize the repairs that he knew needed to happen. It took many, many months. Today, he remains completely healed.

Because of his personal experience, Dispenza was attracted to double-blind scientific studies that used a placebo to measure the effects of a new drug being tested. How is it that those who were given a placebo instead of the new drug were healing?!! Obviously not a one-time occurrence, placebo study results are fairly well-known. While miraculous in appearance, some in the placebo group did experience instantaneous healing. They simply believed they were taking the miracle drug. Many relapsed when they found out they were given the placebo. Dispenza argues we "can be the placebo" with the right attitude and attention . . . and the effects can be permanent. [10]

It is also at this time that I am introduced to a relatively new field of medicine called epigenetics. This, I believe, has been a game changer! Prior to its discovery, most of our scientific models in this area have been based on Newtonian science. Under Newton's Law, we have lived under the premise that we are a product of our genetic material. Our lives are pre-determined by the genes we inherit. For a long time, nothing could change this viewpoint. It is easy to see that, if we are permanently defined by our genetic material, we can conclude there would be little to no opportunity to change our health, our lives, or anything else.

> **Epigenetics is the arm of science that studies the biological mechanisms that switch genes on and off. Environmental stimuli can also cause genes to turn on and off. With more than 20,000 genes at our service, the one thing we can control in this process is the energy we feed our genes. Living on a diet of love and compassion, we hold the power to cure cancer, slow aging, stop obesity, and so much more! [11]**

We replace close to a million cells each day. A telomere forms the "end cap" of each gene. These caps protect the tips of chromosomes when cells divide. Their job is to stop the chromosomes from fraying or sticking to each other. This assures that our DNA gets copied properly when division occurs [12]. Our genes are responsible for signaling new telomere growth at the end of each cell. By studying the physical environment in which new cell growth takes place and by comparing the strength and length of the new telomere compared to one that forms in a different environment, epigenetics teaches *how* new cell growth is *directly* related to the physical environment in which it is growing. This is a big departure from genetic pre-determination!

> **"Individual differences in telomere length have been linked to survival . . . To gain accurate and meaningful estimates of telomere heritability, it is vital that the impact of the environment, and how this may vary, is understood and accounted for." [13]**

What constitutes this "physical" environment? According to Dispenza [14], we learn that the "hormones and elixirs" needed for new cell growth are getting their orders from the brain, which is getting its orders from the emotions and types of stress we are feeding our bodies! Long-term stress, a state that often exists from very old, limiting, and self-denigrating beliefs, is providing instruction for cell growth in this example. If the state of our long-term stress is constant and persistent, telomere growth for new genes is severely compromised. The result is illness . . . disease.

This is a good time to mention that new discoveries occurring in the fields of neuroscience, electromagnetism, and quantum physics are also demonstrating that thoughts can be profoundly creative. All energy transcends matter, even thoughts. I find it interesting that, back in the day, metaphysics had always sought to transcend matter where science spent its time studying it. It turns out that science wins the medal for the most unbelievable and astonishing discoveries. [15]

New cell growth requires energy. A menu of high-level stress, without end, day after day, year after year, will result in disease. What are we feeding our cells? High stress produces stress hormones, and those that accompany fear, anger, envy, greed, et al., are not optimal for cell growth. Sadly, for some, by the time we notice physical suffering in our bodies, it might be too late.

The remedy for optimal physical health is the same for manifestation. Can we change our minds? Can we think new thoughts? What *are* we thinking? We need to pay attention to our thoughts! We also need to decide how badly we want to heal ourselves. What thoughts or attitude can we adopt to intentionally create the right chemical elixir to drive the brain and body from a constant state of stress to a state of healthy cell regeneration? If we can change our minds, we might be able to get another chance at life. [16]

"All of what we are is a result of what we have thought."

—Buddha

So yes, our biology is our biography. Cancer, allergies, tumors, breathing, heart, and all major organ problems are signs that we need to pay attention to our internal environment. We are out of coherence when we meet these challenges. We have the power to change all this with the magic of benevolent and compassionate thinking. I know, from my own personal experience, that with time and practice, I am getting better and better at living in a "state" of joy. Through meditation, I work hard to bring forth elevated emotions and work even harder to keep them inside after meditation is over. I've learned by observing my own reactions to my experiences that I can nip any problems in the bud and work to insure I carry these feelings with me for most of the day. It takes much work, but I can tell you, I have never felt healthier! My arthritis pain, for one, is completely gone. As a candidate for knee replacement surgery five years ago, I can say today that I don't even think about my knees anymore.

I will repeat one last thing about illness because I think about it often. We are not here to die; we are here to heal! Illness, then, is a wake-up call, a big message that we have somehow fallen off the path we have chosen to move in unity with Source. It also buys us time to think about our situation. We get another chance to do it right! We need to pay attention to the messages our bodies are giving us every day, lest we miss the signs!

Energy and Spirituality

I learned that the universe or the quantum field, as defined by the scientists, is an infinite field of knowledge, data, and energy. The universe is also God's playground and as such also holds intelligence, order, and love. Since energy never dies, all those who have passed before as well as angels, guides, and ascended masters remain immortal energetic manifestations of Source. When science highlights the importance of an elevated emotion to heal ourselves or manifest a new life, who is hearing the vibrational frequencies we are sending out? It's those loved ones, angels, guides, and ascended masters! They are the divine intelligence that hears our prayers! They are the ones, through Source, who will work in concert with us to bring joy, love, and compassion to our lives . . . the same emotions that we will apply to a new creation of ourselves. When we pray or meditate for the benefit of ourselves as well as others, we attract a swarm of heavenly helpers to help us get the job done. This is why frequency and vibration are so important. We must make sure that we are heard! To this end, I call upon the Bible for clues on how to get the best results. [17]

There are two Bible quotes that I remember from my early Catholic education: "Ask and you shall receive" and "Let go and surrender." Until I began this work, they held little relevance to me. This was probably due to my inability to understand how to apply these directions to my physical life. When I entered the world of meditation, I uncovered the beautiful truths behind both. Our spiritual helpers out there can't wait to help! I heard this time and time again in my meditation studies. They are filled with love and want to see us grow. If the vibrations and frequencies of our requests match the vibrations and frequencies of the helpers out there, they will swarm to help! Our happiness is all they think about, but they *must* be invited. *We need to ask.* As pure beings, they are all working through the power of God.

The hard part is to let go and surrender! We are cautioned not to be too specific with our requests. We should not attach ourselves to a specific outcome. We need to be careful what we wish for. Why? It might not be in our best interests. Remember there are an infinite number of outcomes. Let our helpers and guides finish the job. In the end, we will get exactly what we need. As long as we continue to do the work, we will be taken care of.

How the universe works is amazing in its logic, its consistency, and its message. I have discovered, time and again, that if I have questions, I will get answers. In the beginning, some answers seemed completely unrelated to the question. The more I delved, however, the more I realized everything I learned was related in some way to what I needed.

We don't always get our questions answered in a logical, linear way. That viewpoint is strictly from the human perspective. From the point of view of the Divine, however, what we do receive makes perfect sense. We will get what we want, though it may manifest in the form of exactly what we need. If we persist, we will discover that. It all comes around in the end.

There is a proper way to ask for help. There is a proper way to communicate with the intelligent energy existing in the universe. There is a proper way to work through our challenges and lessons. Some of it has to do with our approach. All of it has to do with our beliefs, our attitudes, and the store of love, compassion, and forgiveness that must be present for us to understand and change our life. These are the catalysts.

The trouble with emotions is that it often feels like it is something that happens to us . . . but it actually comes from us. That means we are in charge! We have lived with emotions happening to us for so long that we have forgotten we hold the power to form, shape, and control them. I have learned I can change my life with the same emotions I use to experience and understand my life.

Earlier, I talked about past-life regressions and healing miracles. Brian Weiss, MD, author of *Many Lives, Many Masters* [18], and Michael Newton, author of *Journey of Souls* [19], demonstrate the type of healing associated with visiting past lives. The fact that the energy we carried a couple of thousand years ago in another incarnation can still remain with us in this life should be proof enough that we might need to change our point of view as to how things work. Energy never dies. It just changes matter . . . constantly.

The real truth out there is . . . nothing is a secret. The path and the way have been in front of us the whole time. All that's required is desire, awareness, attention, and some joyful feelings about how wonderful our next change will be followed by a willingness to do what comes naturally. We are no different from scientists. Our bodies and our minds are our labs, and our job is to manifest and manage the energy that we invite to create a different and better life.

I saw this in my son. I saw this in myself when I finally put two and two together.

CHAPTER FIVE

The Truth of Creation

Heavenly Hindsight

CREATION! THE WORD ITSELF is just so . . . powerful, yet it doesn't even come close to describing what existence is truly like when the very essence of your soul is immersed in it. Creation occurs everywhere, in every moment and in every time. It is the activity that drives all of us, including the Divine, to participate. It is the reason "To Be."

As a piece of God, we are major creators. We spend most of our living moments creating. We create new ideas, new things, a new way to handle an old problem and new relationships, among a million other possibilities. This is what we do. Our creations match that of the universe in its infinite activity. We are always creating, and to do this, we need to constantly exercise our free will to try new and different approaches. It is only through the application of our will can we learn and create something new.

You will be amazed when you discover for yourself how large creation is in the divine universe. When I arrived at my location in the LBL, the level of energy swirling around creative projects was exhilarating. Depending on their area of interest or expertise, the souls here spend their existence creating new life, new ideas, new plans, new universes, new planets, and more. I am most impressed with those musical souls who are creating new and glorious sounds. It is so musical here! There are choirs of beautiful voices creating new songs, new sounds, and new harmonies. It is all around me. The beauty of Creation is infinite in scope.

There are other souls, like me, whose expertise is in teaching. Teaching from this level is so much more than passing on new truths and new ideas. It involves healing as well as inspiring others to know their souls enough to create new situations that serve both their own highest good as well as that of all who share their essence in this place. A great deal of my activity is spent working with other teachers on teaching projects that will help our earthly brethren understand the challenges they face.

The wonder of what we can do here is so much more expansive than what we can do on earth. For one, it is possible to be in many places at once. My particular skills have already been called into play here to help. Manifestation is through instant thought. We are pure energy here and have access to an endless amount of frequencies with which to create. It is exciting!

It pays to be respectful of our power to create, whether we are doing so from heaven or earth. How well we do this determines how well we live our lives and how happy we will be. It is important to pay attention.

When I started high school, I had finished the first draft of the person I had been creating the prior fourteen years. It seems I painted myself into a bit of a bind. From the journal and with the theme of "friends" as a backdrop, we'll examine the good, the bad, and the ugly of my first major creative effort.

The Mind of Deliberate Creation

When we incarnate on earth, we hit the ground creating. Whether we are aware of it or not, we are creating something every moment of the day. What we create depends on our

motivations, our love of self (or not), our beliefs, and our attitudes. We are not even aware that we are creating. We just think we are "living." This is such an important subject, yet on earth, we have relegated our gift to create to the level of multi-tasking, which is a pretty low level. We don't see ourselves as creators, so we dismiss it. Creating art masterpieces or beautiful symphonies are only one aspect of creation. In the world of our God, creating a loving environment to raise children is held just as dearly as an important piece of art.

Of all of the learning I have undertaken to understand my place here in this life and my "other" life, the one that surprised me the most was the concept of creation and how absolutely hardwired we are to it. As I meander along my journey to understand, I also pick up a new version of the story of creation. This is a little different than our Adam and Eve story, but not so different that I couldn't make the transition to this newer version rather easily. I'll speak to this first.

From my studies of Indian yogis, spiritualists, modern-day doctor/metaphysics, and other people and genres, I come away with a more modern/scientific version of the beginning of life than that described in the Book of Genesis. At its core, the Bible story of Creation is based on truth but delivered in a way that would be understandable to humans at the time. Both versions demonstrate the divine love and power of source.

Source (God) existed in the beginning. Source always was and always will be. But in the beginning, Source decided it wanted to "experience itself." The best way was to create many, many versions of its essence and go out into the universe in order to experience its glories in different ways. This was the beginning of creation. The beauty of this plan is that all of those "versions" Source created to experience itself were pieces of itself. In Catholic grade school, I was taught I was a "reflection" of God. The new version that I recently acquired informs that we are much more than a reflection. We are a piece, an actual "fractal" of Source, where all of the qualities of God reside inside. This includes wisdom, knowledge, pure love, compassion, and more! This was a personal "takeaway" for me and resonated so much more than the story I was taught as a child.

As a child, for some reason, when I heard the Bible story of creation, I created several limiting beliefs about what I had learned. For one, I was angry! Yes, I was angry that we had lost our opportunity to live in paradise for eternity. I was angry that Adam and Eve threw it all away. As a seven-year-old, I thought about this a lot. The effect was a feeling of helplessness that I was forever doomed and it was the fault of Adam and Eve. I carried a "victim mentality" in this regard for most of my elementary school years. I'm sure this was not the intent, but limiting beliefs are insidious, and it's hard to determine how they get "installed." Nevertheless, this experience left me open to other ideas on the beginning of life.

It really doesn't matter if we believe the Book of Genesis or the version I offer above. We all respond differently to varying versions of truth. What matters is that the truth we believe in resonates with us and further inspires us to continue on the divine path laid out for us.

Nevertheless, I never expected creation to be as important as it is. I never viewed myself as a creator. Yes, I understand we are here to learn lessons. I understand that our earthly purpose is to transcend the lessons in front of us and learn them so that we can finally unite with Source. I had a general sense that our overriding purpose in this life and all of our prior lives is to become perfect in love, just like God. I didn't have a problem with the goal at all. It's strange, though, that it never occurred to me that the only way to transform in this way would be through creation.

And yet, when I think about it, I have invested at least twenty years of my life actively reinventing myself. I don't recall ever thinking that I was creating. Humans can be so interesting. We know what creation is, we know what it means, and we know what is involved

. . . when we think about building a structure or producing a work of art. Why is it so hard to imagine we are creating when we decide to change this canvas of our bodies into something new? I have learned that karma in this life is a knapsack of lessons we have carried over to this particular life. Many of these lessons have repeated time and time again. It is assumed we have attempted to clear our debts in prior lifetimes, but sometimes the lessons persist. The entire lesson, including its related bits, must be learned before we can be free of its effects. Coming up with yet another way to deal with the same old problem is enormously creative! Why do we not think to attribute the wonderful aspects of creation to this effort?

How does the urge to create show up in humans? Many times creation is a response to the suffering we are feeling in our lives at any given point in time. In some cases, we may not be aware we are suffering, but we are aware we might be unhappy. Unhappiness is suffering as well and often presents when we wish we were different or had a different life. Finally making the decision to get in shape, for example, is one creative activity most of us have been involved with. We are unhappy because we feel unhealthy and unattractive. We finally commit to a program to change things and create something that we think will work. After a time, we are in good shape, and we want to stay that way. We begin to look at diet and food and proper nutrition. Now we are feeling so good about ourselves that we decide to get a new job! How can this *not* be creative? It is beautifully creative, and the outcome, especially if that new job is in an area we love, can't help but benefit everyone else!

> *"The happiest people don't have the best of everything, they just* make *the best of everything."*
>
> **—Unknown**

So we are creating . . . constantly. It seems this is a pretty important activity and one in which we are always involved. It stands to reason, then, that greater attention to what we are creating every day presents an opportunity to change our lives in profound ways.

So now I am at a point where I learn we aren't just talking about any old kind of creation, but deliberate creation. There is a difference. Remember the Observer Effect in the chapter on energy? Every time we look at something or observe it, we bring it to life. By placing our energy somewhere, we are activating a possibility. We are changing energy! Since we do this all day long, we are essentially creating all day long because we are activating possibilities. For example, you are taking a walk in some beautiful woods. You are seeing many plants and flowers. You observe and move on. You have likely activated something just by seeing the plants in your view, but nothing happens because you move on. Suddenly, you notice a tiny blue flower at the base of a large tree. You stop to look at the flower and imagine how you can pair it with something else. It would look lovely in the entryway. By thinking this thought, you have created a new possibility for these flowers. If you pick them and take them home, you have turned a possibility into a probability. By placing the flowers in a vase in your entryway, you have just created. People who come through will enjoy the bouquet. Now you have benefited others. This is deliberate creation!

Since we have thoughts constantly and we are constantly observing, it pays to use our mind deliberately. Deliberate creation involves identifying a possibility for a new or better life, putting attention and awareness on an outcome that we can deliver to this life, and imagining this outcome with joy and enthusiasm. In the process, others will benefit. This is hard work. No doubt about it. We don't like to change. We like our addictions to habits, emotional or otherwise. There is a certain level of comfort in staying the same. Once we decide, however, to change our minds, we will joyfully experience the miracle of change. There is one more important quality of deliberate creation that must be in place for it to be considered a proper expression of our Godly Source. *Our creations must benefit others as well as ourselves.* This is key. Source loves *all* of us, and from this point of view, all that we create must be of benefit to others as well.

This is one reason why it is important to us to understand the properties of energy better. We need energy to make the changes in our lives we want to make. If we can understand it enough to learn how to effectively manage its direction and outcomes, we will learn how wonderful it is to see our dreams manifest and come to life. I found this aspect of creation so wondrous! Personally, I was excited to manifest a new life. I had this nagging urge to accomplish something after my son died. I needed to find out what that was and then decide how to go about doing it. Long story short, I knew I had to write. I had to manifest myself as a writer whose words could, hopefully, inspire others. This did take a good amount of time, but all of it has been worth it. It goes without saying that the benefits are amazing. Regardless of the outcome, I have learned I am capable of so much! To be in this place right now was something I could not have imagined in the early years. [1]

Lessons, Karma, and Creation

Karma is not about being perfect. It is about self-discovery and realization. It is the story behind the lessons we need to learn in life. Understanding our own personal karma is our big opportunity for growth and transformation.

We are not here to die. We are here to heal. Lessons are the stepping stones to ultimate healing. Karma is the package of lessons we did not learn from prior lives that we bring with us. In energetic terms, both lessons and karma represent an imbalance of energy. Because the universe is perfectly in balance, we must do what we can to readjust those energies and bring them back to normal. Karma is nothing more than an "adjustment," then. Karma is definitely not punishment! It does, however, demonstrate how the Law of

Attraction works. If we are going about our day in a negative way accompanied by low-level emotions, we are going to attract the same energy to us. It is easy to see over time how a build-up of negative energy can become out of balance. This pattern of repeating energy can become our karma, particularly if it isn't cleared in this life. Since the universe communicates via vibrational frequency which contains information, we attract those frequencies that match our own. It's just the way things work. If we aren't happy with our lives and the people and things in it, we are going to have to change our vibration. If we are unwilling to do so in this life, we will carry this energy with us into the next and continue to attract like energy. It will be adjusted sooner or later. Ultimately, we will use our ability to create to change things and, hopefully, our lives.

Creation and the Meaning of Life

Our existence on earth is not a random one. Each and every one of us was planned! Source, in the beginning, designed it so that each of us can bring a new look, a new reality to a universe that is constantly building and changing itself.

When I came across this little bit of an idea, I found myself glowing in "special-ness." I have never felt so . . . wanted! Up until this point, I had been feeling so small, especially in light of the grandeur of all that I was learning. It was hard to imagine how I, personally, could fit into all of this magnificence.

A soul journey is a search for meaning in one's life. We want to know our purpose. Why are we here? Because of our connection to Source and the fact that we *are* Source, it should be pretty clear by now that our most important purpose is creation. We do it anyway all day long just by observing. Recognizing this as our first major calling should help us when we navigate life here on earth . . . and designing a soul journey is enormously creative!!

God has a plan, and he had each of us in mind when he decided to "experience" himself in the beginning. We are necessary for this work for everything that follows depends on us to do our part. This is why, despite our connection to each other and to Source, we are completely unique. We are a "one of a kind" in the entire universe, and it is the energy from our point of view, our thoughts, our actions that gets applied to all the knowledge and wisdom and data the universe has to offer. Our singular viewpoint on existing knowledge is considered new information and is added to the knowledge that already exists. Because our thoughts are exclusive to ourselves (we create them), such viewpoints have never been expressed before. We are actually adding *new* knowledge to the field. We are bringing new life to life.

Dawson Church states, "The concept that mind creates matter is not a metaphysical proposition, it's a biological one . . . this is the material reality of creation." [2] I find it ironic that we humans crave stability when we are changing our world every single second in some way . . . just by observing. Stability is really the absence of change. This just isn't scientifically possible, yet we hang on for dear life.

Our Higher Selves

Our Higher Self is the *holder* of *all* aspects of our consciousness. Our Higher Self is the Grand Creator, Conductor, and Leader of our personal spiritual development. Our Higher Self knows what *all* our other selves are up to. Our Higher Self, which I view as that original spark created by the Divine eons ago, is driven by creation and is constantly looking at new ways and new possibilities to learn all the lessons we need to learn.

Most of us have heard of our higher self. I used to think it referred to the best good that can be done given the immediate situation. Over the years, I have made jokes about checking in with my "higher self" first. This might be a nice conversation filler, but do we really know what our higher self is? Get ready, this is kind of mind-boggling.

Again, many of these answers were derived from recorded past-life regressions from the patients of Brian Weiss and Dawson Church. Specifically this information was gleaned when a past-life regression brought the doctors to the LBL area, where the wisdom of ascended masters and guides, including our higher self, can be accessed. The description of our higher self is so important because it highlights the totality of our true creative power as sparks of the Divine. How we get to know ourselves on earth is extremely limiting, mainly because we have to experience everything through bodies. Our emotions are the intermediary, and the meaning we derive from them depends on how we feel about an experience. Our higher self doesn't have a physical form, so nothing gets "lost in translation." Because of this, our higher selves can be a wonderful source of wisdom and knowledge. If you have a question, ask your heart. This is where our higher self resides. The response will be immediate!

On earth, we only experience aspects of ourselves. When we become incarnate, we do not bring the whole of our spiritual energy with us. We only bring what we need to get the job done. Our physical bodies, as well, couldn't possibly hold the whole of our spiritual essence. So where is the rest of us?

Some of who we are stays in the LBL world, at a much-reduced energy level, of course. There are, however, many, many more aspects of us that are concurrently working on other lessons and activities from other dimensions, other planes of existence, and other time periods. [3] We have a *lot* of lessons to learn. Rest assured, these are *all* aspects of our own unique consciousness. These other beings *are* us! Who's in charge? The higher self! I refer you back to the opening statement of this section.

So we are our higher self here on earth, though at significantly reduced energy levels, and we *are* the full of our higher selves in the field of the Divine. The miracle of understanding this is that any good we do for ourselves on earth will benefit all those other selves working on other self-improvement projects elsewhere. In kind, the work other aspects of ourselves are doing will personally benefit us as well. Our higher self is the whole of what we are personally capable of. This is human creation at its grandest!

A Word on Heavenly Hindsights

I have been given a wonderful gift. The words at the beginning of each chapter, though written by me, were inspired, intuited, gleaned, and derived from my son, who speaks from his heavenly world. Or were they? Are the insights I have stumbled upon from me or from a truly Godly source? I just know that when an answer comes and it resonates deeply in my soul, I know it as truth. Additionally, because I have chosen to believe the answers are divinely generated, I am enormously comforted.

Where does inspiration come from? Those flashes of brilliance that come to people in dreams or visions and which they can't seem to dredge up in a normal conscious waking state are always welcome, surprising, and amazing. But where do they come from? How do we "come upon" this special information that we seek? In the context of this book, I use the term to define the messages I am receiving that seem to keep pointing me in the direction to answers for all of my "why" questions. Since the subject happens to deal with my son's untimely death and I am reaching out to him, I assume the words I am inspired to write are divinely guided. I also sense that the words offered in the beginning of each chapter reveal a level of "experience" I don't recall possessing or remembering. Further, I have never had a vision or life-altering spiritual experience that is often the force behind others who have been deeply inspired. This is the tricky part about soul journeys. We are not always going to get answers or gifts in an obvious and grand way, wrapped in a bow with neon lights flashing.

Most of our answers come quietly, but when they do come, they arrive with surety! We must learn to hear for ourselves and trust our intuition. This is the way the answers come for most of us. Trust that you know so much more than you think you do!

For all intents and purposes, Heavenly Hindsights is a representation that all knowledge is available to all of us, no matter where we are. We are completely connected to the Divine, higher-level souls, and each other, including all those who have lived before. It is our right to access everything the Divine holds. We here on earth just have to earn it, that's all. It might also be a good reminder to know that everything . . . *everything* that has been created on this world had its start in the Divine. Even the great masters of the past seemed to have some awareness of this. It's a humbling thought.

We are also getting messages all the time that reflect thoughts from other sources. Because energy is so malleable and it rushes toward other energy signatures with a vibrational or frequency match, there is a good chance we may get messages or thoughts that might not be directly related to our quest. I call this energy "spillover." These thoughts can come from the Divine and even from other humans. Sometimes we act on these impressions. Lots of times, we don't. If we pay attention, sometimes these other messages can help us. Either way, all of us are infused with Heavenly Hindsight. It can't be helped. It's the way God intended for us to learn and grow. And for us to learn, we must create. Heavenly Hindsight inspires creation!

Patrick had no idea that the divine tools, mentioned above, were available to him to help him navigate his gnarly high school years. I certainly didn't know they were available. It is at times like this that I wished my faith had encouraged me to look within for divine answers instead of to a dogma of rules pertaining to behavior. I can recite a list of mortal and venial sins that I was charged not to commit. None of this was very comforting. Despite his challenges, Patrick nevertheless had some very shining moments in his short life. He had his dark times, too, but it's funny, I really only reminisce about the good.

The Journal: High School

By the time I entered high school, I had the basics of an identity. I was one of the "cool" bad boys. My "back of the classroom" antics continued as an important aspect of my repertoire. I could make people laugh, but oftentimes it was at someone's expense . . . any one of my friends (who just laughed at me) or some poor, nerdy soul who inadvertently happened on our path. I created this diversion in middle school because it worked. I became the center of attention for a moment, and it made (some) people like me. There was no reason to change this for high school.

At the same time, I discovered I had a good number of talents and gifts that I came to appreciate in later years. I was so busy tending to my friends that I didn't spend much time studying. It took up too much time. I had the ability, however, to keep my grades up to a certain level because not doing so just drew attention to my not-so-attractive "other life." It was definitely a balancing act, and it took a lot of energy to maintain.

School was a drag, though. I sucked at algebra, math, and Spanish . . . too much memorization. I loved English, history, computer science, and speech. These areas of study came really easy for me and required little effort. My rotten grades in the sciences and language were offset by my stellar grades in the other subjects. Without much effort, I had an average GPA of about 2.9, good enough to stay in school!

I was particularly good at writing and won a number of awards. My most impressive win was in sophomore year when I submitted for a nationwide teen writing contest on the sports industry sponsored by USA Today. Highly inspired by Mom and Dr. Laura Schleshinger, a radio talk show personality at the time who offered hard advice over the air to those who called in and to whom Mom listened incessantly, my article was about the responsibilities athletes carry as role models for young people. My submission would be one of the two that won the contest and earned publication in the paper. Praise, high fives, congratulations, and even fan mail were heaped on this humble effort. These were glory moments that created temporary diversions from my day-to-day behavior and for which I was grateful.

Sophomore year was an excellent year for the communication arts in general. I also came in as one of two finalists in the speech contest held that year. This was a semester project, which consisted of writing the speech and practicing its presentation. Presentations were made first to sophomores in order to whittle the field to just a handful of students who made their final presentations to the entire student body. I earned the nickname "The Senator" because I kept adjusting my eyeglasses as I paced back and forth. I came in second because of this, but the moniker I earned was the prize I really cherished!

My participation in team sports died in my freshman year. I gave wrestling a go, but I just wasn't aggressive enough to win. Not in the DNA. Despite all the troubles I had in life, I was never violent. Hurting people physically never occurred to me. Either way, I was one of the lucky ones who didn't have to worry about keeping my weight down to qualify for a lighter class. I was naturally skinny to begin with, and my escalating experimentation with drugs didn't help matters.

I gave up inline skating to take on snowboarding. I did this most weekends with Eric, my best friend at the time, and a few others. It was on these trips that my experimentation with drugs and drinking grew legs. The effect on my day-to-day life at the time was not evident. Further, I was too young to know that there is a line that can be crossed when getting high. In my freshman and sophomore years, it was no harm, no foul.

While high school offered much in the way of new experiences, many of them good, it is easy to see how my obsession with having friends still played prominently in my planned development.

I had created a persona that would allow me to continue to explore but at the same time fill that need for friends that had been plaguing me since daycare. There were times when I could have made a different choice. I wasn't usually high during the day when I was in school, and if I had looked carefully, I would have discovered that there were a lot of people that liked me. I had the opportunity to look at friendship in a different way, but I chose not to. Rather, my beliefs about how to have friends had begun to focus, instead, on using relationships. Somehow, I had crossed the line, thereby creating a glaring lesson that I would painfully have to face a few years later.

Things changed when I turned sixteen, entered junior year, and got my driver's license. We lived in a country-like area that was about five miles from school. There were no buses where we lived, so I was given our old car to drive to school. I would also drive my sister to school, and I spent a lot of time running errands for Mom. But I had wheels! I had freedom! It was an acceptable trade-off.

Ever vigilant, Mom noticed how much free time I had on my hands after I quit wrestling. Now that I had a car, she decided I would apply that free time to get a job. I didn't argue too much because I needed the money, both for drugs and the car. I used the counseling office to look at job postings and checked it frequently. It only took a couple of weeks before I found the job of my dreams . . . Autodesk!! Local. Computers. Good pay and fun!

It is no accident that the Autodesk job showed up on the board when it did. My interest in computers had been thriving and growing since I was five years old. I was creating a life around this very important thing. Coincidence and synchronicity are components of creation. My perpetual love for computers attracted like energy from all possibilities available to me. It's not surprising that I just happened to be in the right place and the right time for this job to present itself. Like does, indeed, attract like!

At the time, Autodesk was working on design templates for architects, designers, and others. All those coding years of playing *Dungeons and Dragons* made the Autodesk work easy-peasy. It was actually a little too easy. I worked on a team with others of my ilk, and we were given work assignments and project goals to complete. I usually worked after school from three p.m. to six p.m. The work we were given took a nanosecond to complete. I don't think Autodesk knew how easy it was. After we finished our work, we, you guessed it, played computer games against each other until closing time. Life didn't get any better!

I was lucky. I had a gift for programming. I recognized it early on when I was a kindergartener learning to write from a computer in the library. Sometimes in this life, we are offered such gifts. They are major hints as to our true purpose in this life and offer an attractive option for how we can live in the earth plane. This was one gift I didn't let go to waste. I engineered much of my "non-using" time in the pursuit of computers and everything they involved. In the short time I had in life, I can say I did not squander this ability. I just made sure to fit it in with everything else.

Life can be so surprising. Below is a story that demonstrates how my ability with computers and my continual need to be disruptive joined together to create a new opportunity for me. It's important to look for grace in the most unusual places.

In my junior year, I was popular. While still characterized inside a relatively benign group of troublemakers, my posse continued to delight in back-of-the-classroom antics that everyone, except the teacher, thought was hysterical. This usually happened in science class, where there was more opportunity to roam. When this mood hit me, my "punishment de jour" was to be ejected from the classroom and sit out the period in the library . . . which suited me just fine.

One day, I sauntered over to the library on one of those "Patrick, go to the library" days. I liked going to the library because I had access to all the computers. On this particular day, I saw a buddy of mine, also on classroom detention. It was like a party in detention!

I sat down at a computer and glanced over at the librarian. This day she was wearing her extra-heavy eyeglasses as she peered unblinkingly at her computer. I told my buddy, "Watch this." I turned to my keyboard and entered a few critical keystrokes, hit enter, and then directed my friend to watch the librarian.

As she was working diligently on her computer, her face took on an ashen gray color. In slow motion, her expression morphed into a look of horror and disbelief. I knew what was happening. Her computer screen was emptying itself of everything she had been working on. To see her reaction was pure bliss. After a few minutes, she looked so distraught; I actually felt a tiny bit of shame at what I had done. So I got up, meandered over her way, and asked her if everything was all right.

"Nooooooo!" she wailed. "I don't know what's wrong with my computer! All my work has disappeared!"

"Let me take a look." She gave me her seat, and with a little extra flourish added to my keystrokes, I restored everything for her. Her gratitude was over the top.

That day I left classroom detention a hero. Word of my good deed spread across the campus, and I was praised high and low. While none of this changed my behavior in science class, it did create a new reputation for me as a computer guy, a title of which I was quite proud.

Okay. That is one example of creation at work. It is actually a better example of like attracting like, which continues the creative effort, but this is not what we mean by "deliberate creation." In contrast, the next story I tell is my best work at deliberate creation.

My Journey to Understand:
Synchronicity and Coincidence

It is easy to see how Patrick's interests led him to imagine building a life around them. Even when the original intent wasn't particularly benevolent, he could still create a different experience that supported the overriding objective. Patrick's interest in computers provides the perfect example. Here we learn a bit of the process that divine creation employs to help us manifest our dreams. Here we learn how important synchronicity and coincidence are toward our creative efforts.

Synchronicity and coincidence are the wonderful byproducts of creation at work. As we make choices with our minds, resonant energy fields synchronize themselves and come together to produce a specific outcome. While the plan is still a work-in-progress, these energy fields produce byproduct as a result of what is being created. What is this byproduct? They are the synchronicities and coincidences that just happen to come our way and also just happen to give us exactly what we need to know right now in the life we are creating. [4]

> **Coincidences provide us with just the right information, just the right person, just the right place, and just the right thing to assist in our personal evolution. They keep us on the path of creation. None of them are random or accidental. There is only order in the Divine field.**

Often called "Pennies from Heaven," the synchronicities that come to us are the signs that our plan is being worked on! They are regular reminders that we are being observed and helped by greater minds. They are the messages that what we will get will be exactly what we need.

"Synchronicity is God's way of remaining anonymous."

—Albert Einstein

The following demonstrates a personal example of synchronicity in my own life. A little while ago, we were experiencing a little financial crunch. It was really no big deal, but I kept thinking if I had an extra thousand dollars or so, we could get over the hump. I didn't put a lot of energy into this effort because things usually work out, but I thought about it from time to time. A short time later, I received a letter from the University of Delaware, where our daughter graduated from college. In the letter was a check for thirteen hundred dollars for an overpayment of tuition. *Lauren had graduated five years earlier!* Coincidence? Yes. A random coincidence? No! We got the money when we needed it.

Dawson Church, in his book *Mind to Matter*, states, "The universal field is an intelligent field of energy where all possibility exists. To encourage synchronicity, a component of creation, we can deliberately entrain our local minds to the non-local consciousness of the universe in which the spontaneous coordination of nature is ever present." [5]

This is a lot bigger than just wishing for an outcome. Synchronicity comes after we have made a deliberate choice to change something. It comes after we have decided that the change we want to happen not only benefits us, but serves the greater good as well.

And just like everything else on the journey we might be taking on, we must *Pay Attention!* If we don't, we might miss the signs. In my case, it's the signs that keep me motivated. They are exciting to find, and it's pretty easy to figure out what they are related to. They are the divine "pat on the back," the encouragement we need to keep going.

Clearly Patrick's interest in computers and how he would use them in his life was developing into an impressive creation. Because of his interest, he came across many opportunities to work his computer magic. The story from the library is just one of them. The difference in the Autodesk job and the library "incident" shows the difference between creation and deliberate creation. The Autodesk job clearly indicates potential for the higher good. The library "creation" was the result of we call "free choice." We learn more about this in the chapter on free will. Free choice is just doing what you want in the moment. It is not the same as free will, which is a deliberate choice to create something that can provide beneficial change for all. It was no accident that Patrick found the Autodesk job exactly when he needed it.

Many of the personal creations Patrick planned for himself in high school became fully realized. His work with Team Xbox is one example. To be honest, I was quite impressed to see how he managed to combine all of his passions, past and present, into this work. At the time, I considered it somewhat advanced for someone of his age. Of course, neither of us would know that Patrick had such a short time to live. Given this, it makes some sense that he would have the pleasure of experiencing something that it might take the rest of us a lifetime to develop.

> *"The most fulfilled people I know—world-famous creatives, billionaires, thought leaders, etc., look at their life's journey as 25% finding themselves as 75% creating themselves."*
>
> —Tim Ferris

The Journal: Team Xbox

When a body dies too young, one wonders if that is possibly enough time to make a contribution to the world. I spent the last year of my life as a staff writer for Team Xbox. Now maybe you might wonder, how is this significant?

First, I discovered that I was able to combine everything I loved to do into one venue. Writing, skating, sports, and computers were all I really thought about. Since I had grown up with computers, I was able to comfortably adapt to the rapidly advancing technology at the time, particularly in the area of game play. As a kid, I cut my teeth on Mario Brothers and later on Nintendo. It didn't take long for me to master most of the games and levels. I had been at it half my life . . . a long time for most people.

I still played *Dungeons and Dragons* but was having difficulty with the code at very high game levels. I needed new tools!

One day Mom was making a trip to the bookstore and asked me if I wanted her to bring anything home. Perfect! I gave her a list of programming manuals to buy, C++, HTML, and Fortran. Mom was stunned. She didn't even know there were such things. She actually thought I was going to give her a list of reading books for school to buy. She came home with three fat books with all the code in the world that I would need for my games. She never knew she was an unwilling mule of knowledge that would support my *Dungeons and Dragons* habit. Nevertheless, she was impressed. I guess I was kind of a complicated guy.

When the Xbox was introduced, it boasted super-cool graphics, audio, sound effects, game levels, and more. Microsoft was producing the early software for these games. As much as I enjoyed coding, playing games in a simulated "real" environment was exhilarating.

I became obsessed and had to have an Xbox. They were absolutely impossible to find. Everyone wanted one! The "wait list" for ownership was months long. I was driven but didn't know how to get my hands on one. They were also expensive, but I would deal with that later. It became a mission of sorts.

My constant nagging on the subject started to irritate Mom. The holidays were around the corner and she, unbeknownst to me, took it upon herself to do the impossible and somehow score an Xbox for me for Christmas. Her little journey took her to numerous stores and many inquiries. In the most coincidental of circumstances, a conversation with our rug cleaner on the subject revealed he worked part time at an electronics store and they had those Xboxes in stock but were waiting to put them on the floor. They knew there would be mayhem the minute the word got out. Our rug guy told Mom to come by the day before the rest of the world would know they had them. He would put one aside for her. I was more than surprised to see that Xbox under the tree. I couldn't imagine how she did it.

Indeed! Synchronicity and manifestation at work! When we place attention on something in a positive way, we influence the energy that surrounds us in a positive way. Having an Xbox, for me, was as important as fulfilling my life's purpose. We all have the power to manifest. The signs that the universe has your back are the synchronicities and coincidences that come our way. They are not random, miraculous events, though they certainly seem to be when they occur. They are simply the result of using positive thoughts with a positive emotion to change one's life for a higher good. Scoring that Xbox was perfect synchronicity in action!

Playing computer games with a graphic interface was so cool. I won't say I was addicted to Xbox because I was too busy, but when I did play, it was always Xbox. I reached some very high levels in the game, and as a result, I noticed there were some weaknesses in the programming. An online search revealed that Microsoft had a Team Xbox website where you could send in comments. I started sharing my thoughts under the pen name Delvael. Within a few months, I was asked if I was interested in being an official staff writer and contribute on a regular basis. I wouldn't get paid, but I would be sent new games to review as soon as they came out!

My game reviews were long. We had to comment and rate four key areas of the game: gameplay, graphics, longevity, and next-gen rate. I created an approach for a consistent review that included an opinion and a conclusion for storyline, graphics, gameplay, and audio. For each area after a written review of the category, I would suggest a rating from between one and five. Readers had an opportunity to comment on the review and suggest their own ratings.

My first review was *The Simpsons: Road Rage* written on January 11, 2002. I was seventeen years old. My last review on *Unreal Championship* was delivered on November 20, 2002. All told, I completed twelve full reviews.

Here's a sample of the opening paragraph for the review I did on *Jet Set Radio Future* (JSRF) on February 19, 2002.

"Strap on the skates and prepare to stretch your imagination as Sega unleashes its out of this world sequel to the hit Jet Set series. Smilebit, the remote developing studio working under Sega responsible for Jet Set Radio Future, has outdone themselves yet again. Outfitted with an uncanny craving for unique style and originality, this developing appendage offers what few can. Get ready to bob your head to the funky fresh beats and absorb the hip new flavor that isn't available on any other Xbox game. One of a kind gameplay, exceptional cell shaded graphics, and exclusive soundtracks topped off with a colossal replay value are only a handful of things that make this game a prodigy in its own time. If you were a fan of the original Jet Set Grind on Dreamcast, then welcome home. For those of you who haven't had the privilege of hopping onto the bandwagon with the current heap of Jet Set's ghetto fabulous cronies . . . I suggest you pay your way. Warning! This game is not for those who suffer from motion sickness, are faint of heart or prone to seizures. Jet Set Radio Future travels in the one way fast lane toward gaming greatness and shall be the catalyst for all games to come that bear new and original ideas."

The following excerpt from a later review I wrote for Gravity Games shows the connection between my middle school inline skating days and my passion for continuing the sport in the virtual world. It's nice to link your pleasures with your work.

"Ever since that magical moment when I discovered aggressive inline skating, I became a hardcore extreme sports fanatic. There was no distance I would not travel to grind the Holy Grail of all rails or to find the utopia of skate parks. I had a sweet passion for the sport and tended to have a slight bias against those other 'extreme' skateboarders and bikers. Alas, I was young and did not give them the respect they deserved. But as I matured to the ripe age of fourteen, I realized my body was too old and brittle to continue putting myself through so much injury. I hung up my skates and picked up the remote control, where I could tune in to ESPN2 and watch my favorite extreme hobbies on X Games and Warped Tour at a safe distance. It was at this time I paid special close attention to the vert and street bikers. I was in awe at the skill and height these riders had. Watching them nearly drew me into the sport itself . . . almost. Luckily enough for my battered self, I was able to participate in another medium . . . video games!"

There was a greater benefit to being a staff writer for Team Xbox than just free games. Team Xbox had created a reputation in the gaming world of being a professional and reliable critic in a world dominated by virtual danger, violence, skill, and game play. As a result, they were tightly linked in with new and old game developers who needed experts to try out their games. Welcome to the world of the launch party!

This was the beginning of the millennium, and San Francisco was becoming a hub of high tech. Any developer worth its salt wanted to host their launch parties in the San Francisco Bay Area. These were heady affairs at fine restaurants and convention centers where those of us who resided in the virtual world could finally meet each other and team up for new gameplay in an indulgent, lush environment. Even better, we were able to rub elbows with the creators, developers, and distributors of the games. The gaming world is a lot smaller than I thought. The ability to meet, greet, and chit-chat opened up a whole new world for me, *and* for the first time in my life, I had an unlimited cache of new friends.

Product reviews, launch parties, and game play all came together in preparation for the big guns, an E3 Expo scheduled in Los Angeles for May 2002. This was a massive meetup of game developers and more at the L.A. convention center. Team Xbox had a booth, and I was invited to attend as a Team Xbox representative. I was over the moon when I got the call to participate in the early spring of that year. The only problem was I needed to be eighteen years old to attend. No date for the event was given when I was invited, so it was a nail biter. I would turn eighteen on May nineteenth. The date was finally announced. E3 was scheduled for one week later. I would be eighteen for one week by the time I got to go!

Another awesome creatively induced synchronicity!

Rehab

Despite these shining moments, my drug use escalated. The summer just before my junior year and just after I got the car was when I experimented with hallucinogens, such as mushrooms and the feel-good drug ecstasy. I also discovered girls the prior year, which was another drug of sorts. Life was good that summer. Parties! Freedom! Money! Car! It was also the time when I officially finalized my creation of drug user, but I wasn't aware of that at the time.

I drank more at parties than I used to, and I started drinking at home when I was alone. Mom and Dad would venture out for dinner and a movie, and after they left, I hit the vodka bottle. One time they got home and found me with my head in the toilet bowl disengaging my guts. Upon the requisite subsequent interrogation, I lied through my teeth. I was in panic mode. Sadly, this was not enough to deter my activities. I resolved to be sneakier.

So now we have a perfect creation of drug user and liar, whose attributes I had been nurturing since my Edward years.

In the glorious "safe time" between report cards, I continued with my previously established activities, none of which matched what anyone else had in mind. I continued to play *Dungeons and Dragons,* but the levels got really difficult by this time.

Mom was not happy with the amount of time I was spending online, so she attempted to restrict my efforts in this area. To counterattack this ridiculousness, I decided to go downstairs at midnight to play. Oftentimes, I didn't get to bed until about four a.m. This was clearly not a recipe for success.

Over time, the lack of sleep and extracurricular activities took their toll. My grades had slipped badly. I looked like crap and was extremely uncooperative. Mom had had it! The war was on.

It started with the directive to meet me at our doctor's office after school one day. Unfortunately, I chose that day to indulge in a few tokes at lunchtime and, as a result, forgot about the appointment.

Now, Mom is like a pit bull when she gets stuck on something. We didn't have cell phones in those days, just pagers, and mine was about to explode. I had to get to a phone to call her. Needless to say, she was furious, and when she arrived to pick me up, she knew immediately that I was stoned. It didn't matter. She took me to the doctor anyway . . . and of course brought up my drug use. I didn't say much in that appointment.

The next thing I knew, I was sitting in a psychologist's office.

I actually liked my psychologist. Her name was Jennifer, and she was very nice. She was probably a little too nice, because I never told her anything revealing. She told Mom I was delightful. Since she never really delved, I considered the hour a nice time to chat. Oh, we talked about "safe" things, but when it came to drugs, I only admitted to recreational use. After about six weeks or so, I totally blew it.

I was a few months away from eighteen, would soon be an adult, and there was nothing anybody would be able to make me do. My mom's antennae were on full alert. She watched me like a hawk. And, in my stupidity, I was in a chat room with one of the internet game players I spent the rest of my time with, and we got to talking about drugs.

Now, this dude was hardcore! He was using stuff I had never heard of before. I pretended I knew what he was talking about and had a conversation about our "shared experiences" . . . then left the damn thing open on my computer for the world to see . . . mainly Mom. She swept in like a tornado, and I was caught in the vortex . . . not the eye, where it is calm and serene, but smack dab in the middle of a massive whirlwind.

She printed the entire conversation and then, unbeknownst to me, made an appointment to see Jennifer and showed her the printout. Mom didn't say much to me about this whole incident for about a week or so. This was uncharacteristic, and I was a little bit concerned.

This concern would later prove to be well-deserved. One random day, a little bit later, I was running errands with Mom, and she told me I would be starting rehab in a week. It would last for nine months.

Nine months!!! It was the tail end of my junior year. This meant it would impact my entire summer and the better part of my senior year. My mom, my "watcher," my annoyance, my warrior, and my savior, slapped me in rehab my senior year! This just sucked big time. But, you know, I couldn't get mad. I wondered, well, maybe I do need help. I was only seventeen, so of course I had no say in the matter. No use fighting it. Anyway, it would be something new.

Now, there are a lot of rehabilitation places Mom could have picked. This is Marin County, home of glorious rehab centers . . . beautiful grounds, hikes, walks, gentle therapy, etc. etc. This is *not* the kind of place she selected. Instead, she found a hole-in-the-wall outpatient clinic run by former addicts with degrees who saw through my bullshit pretty quickly. It was an AA-based program that treated the entire family. According to Mom, addiction is a family affair.

Sometimes the dynamics of a family create just the right situation for one of the members to start using. Our family was one. Both of my parents had a great education, meeting at UCLA. Both were professionals. Both were intelligent, but Dad had the edge on IQ, I think. He's a cerebral thinker with a gift for computers and software, which I happily inherited. IQ isn't everything, though. Mom had intuition, paid attention, was aware, and worked furiously to keep me on the straight and narrow. She also could see right through me. Mom was going to be in charge of this rehab event, because Dad wouldn't talk about it. He never objected, though. So, yes, Mom was going to get to be the "bad guy" once again. I really didn't like her very much in those days.

Things started off pretty well. Therapy was new for all of us. My little sister was only in sixth grade and didn't always come to our therapy sessions. I wish she had. But she was young and really didn't understand. I still wish she came.

All stops were pulled in the charm department during my first meeting with a therapist. I was articulate and funny. I was smart. I liked to talk, so silence wasn't a problem. I planned my first visit strategy carefully and walked out of that session convinced I wouldn't be in this program for nine months.

When my mom talked to my therapist afterward, he told her he found me "slick." Whoa! Not expecting that. What is slick? Like a used car salesman? What did he see . . . except right through me? This did not portend a happy result.

Nevertheless, the die was cast. It looked like I might be here a little longer than I thought.

The first month or two were actually pretty cool. I was clean for the first time in ages, and I felt good. I still enjoyed my job at Autodesk, and my GPA was recovering. The deeper I got into therapy, however, the harder it got. The worst news during this time was that I would have to give up my friends.

I objected heavily to this dictate. The friends I struggled so hard to get in the beginning were now destined for . . . the outbox? Well, we'll see. I spent my lifetime working on friends. I would not give them up easily. Doing drugs with them, however, was going to be problematic. I needed to figure out something else.

The schedule was intense. The family and I were all assigned the same therapist. I had one private session a week with my therapist, and we had one family session a week. I had to attend a group meeting of my peers once a week, and we had to attend a peer group family meeting once a week. So far, that's four sessions for me a week and two for my family. In addition, I had to attend four AA meetings a week. My mom and dad had to attend at least one Ala-non meeting a week. The scorecard is now eight sessions a week for me and a minimum of three for Mom and Dad. The sessions were scheduled for after school and/or work and the early evenings.

I didn't tell any of my friends what was going on. I was too embarrassed. Mom didn't tell anyone in her family. She was embarrassed, too.

Did I mention there was random drug testing? We never knew when or how often this would happen. It could be three times a week or we could skip a week. Hmmm. There are ways to fake tests. Even though I had never been drug tested before, I knew all about how to escape detection. Of course all of the counselors knew the tricks that masked relapses as well . . . dilution, switching urines samples, etc. Why would that not have occurred to me?

I had a heavy schedule with school, work, and now my rehab responsibilities. It didn't occur to me at the time that all those rehab and AA meetings would really cut into my social life. It wasn't apparent to my friends until a month or so later when they realized they hadn't seen me for a while and they missed me. Fortunately, I was a good liar, so I held them off for a little while longer.

The first few months in rehab were actually not too bad. As it often is when I'm faced with new things, I put my best foot forward. Things go well until they get hard or I get bored, and such was the case over the summer and the first few months of my last year in high school. Besides, I got to like the kids in my peer group. It seemed we had a number of things in common, aside from using. I followed all the rules in those early days, including attending all four AA meetings a week and getting my card signed off by the moderator.

After a time, my friends stopped bugging me to hang with them. They bought the line that work, hard classes, and other duties kept me occupied. We still caused a little trouble in those math and science classes, but now everyone, including the students, ignored us. Further, most of us were still preparing for SATs and thinking about college applications and visits, so truly, time was at a premium.

By Christmastime, the bloom was off the rose. I had been in rehab for about six months. I had only three months more to go. I actually started slipping pre-Thanksgiving. A few tokes at a party and, of course, the "safer" drinking choice were part of my strategy to get through the last final, gruesome months. Drinking was safe because it wasn't the sort of thing they tested for at rehab. The pot was a different story. I attempted to disguise my use with diluted urine, borrowed urine kept warm, and so on and so forth. Rehab gave me the benefit of the doubt by asking me to take the test a little later.

After a few weeks of this, it did come up in our family therapy session. Mom and Dad were sorely disappointed. My counselor explained that relapses were to be expected. Mom was skeptical. I resolved to get better at hiding my dastardly deeds.

Things were going okay at home despite this setback. Let me put it this way. I was behaving well outwardly but very sneaky behind the scenes.

One night I was downstairs working on the big computer when Mom popped in to see what I was up to. The timing couldn't have been worse. I was working on making fake IDs. One of my buddies at rehab and me got to talking about how cool it would be to have fake IDs but upon investigation discovered they were out of our price range. I was convinced I could make them myself. He gave me the driver's license of someone of age, and I went to work on it.

Mom came in all perky just to say hey and then saw what I was doing. The gear shift between perky and super pissed-off was instantaneous. She grabbed the license and the fake ID I was working on and snorted, "This looks like crap. You'd never get away with this. If you're going to do something illegal, at least make it look professional!" It appeared this was her new tactic. She didn't scream and yell much anymore, deciding instead to rat me out to the counselors so they could shame me in their own way . . . which was a lot more effective. And that is exactly what she did.

This was, indeed, a pretty stupid thing to do. Not only did I get busted, but now there was another family involved, since their son was my partner. We were the topic of discussion at peer group meetings, family group meetings, and, naturally, in all of my counseling sessions. Despite my perfect expression of "cool," I was rattled. I did not like to be singled out this way, and I especially didn't like to have to answer for my actions publicly. After the whole thing blew over, I resolved to be smarter. I also considered just sticking to the program. I backed off on the extracurriculars for a while just to create some space and calm things down.

I did okay, but I wasn't really committed to "old news" rehab anymore. Still, it was a hassle to sneak around. I decided to plug through until I was released from the program, but I didn't like it. My attitude reflected that decision. I became uncommunicative, surly, and kind of mean. Rehab is stressful. What can I say? This lasted about seven weeks or so . . . until the next incident.

Now this next thing had nothing to do with drugs or anything illegal, which really ticked me off. I was out with a school buddy, non-user, at lunch time, and I ordered one of my usual thirty-ounce sodas. On the way back to campus, we were on the freeway overpass, and I tossed my half-empty soda drink out the window. There was a pedestrian walking on the narrow walkway, and the drink landed right in front of him, completely soaking him. I didn't really aim for him, but then I didn't "not" aim for him, either. When he got dunked, I thought it was hysterical. I got back to school and forgot the incident.

That afternoon when I got home, I decided to take a nap. The doorbell rang, and I heard my mom answer it. Within a minute or so, she came into my room and said, "Oh, Patrick, the police are here for you." Shit.

The officer was in the entryway when I came out. The first thing he did was read me my rights. He didn't even introduce himself. What the hell was this? Either way, I didn't lose my cool. Then he told us that a woman driving behind us had witnessed the assault on this poor pedestrian. She took the license number of my buddy's car, and the cop had already been to his house. He gave the cop my name, and so here we are. He asked me what happened.

Normally, in a situation like this, I would have lied. Lying has served me so well over the years. A lot was going through my head at the time, and for some reason, I decided to tell the truth. Good decision! The cop told me if I had lied, he would have arrested me. Instead, he told me that I was on his radar and from here on out, he would be on hyper alert if he ever discovered I was involved in some nefarious activity. He would be watching me.

Okay. That was scary. Following this was another round of family group and peer group meetings when my mom volunteered this information for discussion and public shaming.

Only about a month to go, then I would be free!

Well, I wouldn't exactly be free ... I needed to get into college first. That was the ticket. Subsidized and financed freedom! My SAT scores were not much better in my senior year than my PSAT scores were in my junior year. They weren't bad, just middle of the pack, but I didn't have that 4.0 GPA to offset the mediocre test scores. I had managed to get my overall GPA up to about a 3.3, which should be enough to get me into a Cal State university.

I was accepted to San Jose and San Francisco State. I was waitlisted for Chico. It was also April, and I would be done with rehab in a few weeks. I planned to have a glorious summer.

Mom didn't seem excited that my rehab was ending. I would also be eighteen in May and an adult. She wouldn't be able to make me do anything I didn't want to do. Did I ever mention not to underestimate Mom?

The fighting started up again at home due, in large part, to my occasionally tumbling grades and in major part because of my surly temperament. I still had time to salvage my grades, but I was thinking about my future and all the good times coming. I finally got a late acceptance from Chico and couldn't wait to go there! Life was good . . . until the final talk.

As part of the rehab program, our family was offered pro-bono psychiatrist visits in addition to all of the counseling we were getting at rehab. The psychiatrist was called in early to determine if I suffered from depression or some other mental disorder. I did not, but the visits were good.

It was a little different talking to a real shrink and especially one who did not have a history of drug abuse in his past. I was treated as a unique individual with unique problems. When you get therapy for drug use from ex-drug users, therapy is from the perspective that they know goes on in the user's head . . . kind of generic. It was effective, but I really didn't think I was a true addict like everyone else . . . just a borderline addict who still had control over his choices. I liked talking to the doctor. He was a cool guy, and it wasn't lost on me that he donated his services. My mom really liked him, too, and it was with him that she shared her latest concerns.

When Mom arranged for us to have another "talk," she had already planned, in concert with my shrink, a new strategy for me. She told me she was proud of me for completing the program. She acknowledged it was hard, but she also said that my attitude the prior month or so was very distressing. She also told me she feared three months of summer vacation with no rehab or AA would wipe out all the good that was gained in the prior year.

Therefore, as soon as I graduated from high school, she would like me to go to a six-week Wilderness Quest Rehab program in Utah, recommended by our shrink. She felt I needed one more big dose of rehabilitation before I went to college to make sure that all I had learned would "set" and "gel." She was not confident, based on my behavior, that I was truly dialed in to what a drug-free life meant. She told me the choice was mine.

Excellent.

She also told me that if I did not go to this program the summer before college that I would need to move out of the house when I graduated, get a job, and find a place to live and support myself . . . just in case my Chico acceptance was rescinded. If I was going to die from using drugs, she didn't want to watch me do it. I would have to be on my own. Dad offered up the military as an option and told me he had made an appointment to see an army recruiter.

A lot happens behind the scenes when you are not paying attention.

Needless to say, I was beyond angry. I felt trapped. This was extortion! I would hate my mom and maybe dad for life. Nevertheless, I had to decide.

Not one to exert too much energy in any one direction, I concluded it would be best to go. It was only six weeks, after all, and then I would be moving off to college. I reckoned I could deal with it. My life hadn't been my own for a year now. What's six weeks? But I didn't have to be pleasant about it, and I wasn't. I was able to maintain my GPA.

Finally, it was graduation time. Senior grad night, senior day, awards banquets, college acceptance announcements . . . all were cool activities that marked our rite of passage. Even though I applied about a seventy-five percent effort on average throughout high school, I still got accepted to three colleges, and I was off the Chico waitlist!

For some strange reason, despite the unpleasant news that I was going to summer rehab, I became more committed to my sobriety. I really did work hard to get out of high school with my grades and behavior intact. Dad and I had an interview with an army recruiter and military life was not for me. On the other hand, I wasn't willing to move out of the house to get a job without a degree. It looked like Mom's ultimatum was going to be the path I took. I might as well prepare for it.

I managed to get through all the end-of-year parties with minimal damage. There were one or two times when I slipped up a bit, but a beer here or there, given the circumstances, represented a huge improvement over where I had been a year earlier. I never felt better in my life. I was still angry, though, and carried a sour disposition at home.

I was scheduled to leave for Utah one week after graduation. I turned eighteen a few weeks before graduation. Mom got in contact with Edward and asked him to come over on my birthday weekend to surprise me with a visit. Edward and I went out that night, and on a lark, I asked him if he wanted to smoke some pot. He turned me down. I guess too many years had come between us. At first I thought Edward had changed, but later, I realized it was me. I felt a bit ashamed, but it was still good catching up with him. I would only see him one more time before I died.

My Journey to Understand

While this section of Patrick's journal highlighted his manifestation efforts, the attitude he carried with his friends continued along the "using" relationships timeline. He had not yet made the connection between how he viewed his relationships with friends and his drug use. Despite his successes, he still retained those limiting beliefs about friends that I had imprinted on him during his daycare years. His high school accomplishments were impressive, but they didn't help him see that he wasn't different from anyone else. He still carried this with him. As mentioned earlier, this was one of my primary childhood problems.

It took me about forty years to figure out that my thoughts on friendships were limiting beliefs. Had I paid attention, I would have seen the causal effect on my son's life. This wasn't his problem. He had a completely different childhood than I did. There was nothing about his life that would have prevented him making good friends. In my effort to be a "good mother," I didn't want my son to suffer in the same way I had, but first I had to create the problem for him so that I could then make him aware of it.

One really needs to be careful with what we teach our children. They absorb everything and become like sponges. In order for Patrick to understand this at age three, he had to somehow create a friendless environment for himself. Now he understood!

Truth be told, I have since discovered that I didn't really have a problem with friends, either. My childhood was one of criticism and a sense I was unlovable. What this really meant was I did not love myself. Criticism can do that to children. It creates an inability to love oneself. When we possess little or no self-love, it is difficult to believe that anyone anywhere will find us likable.

The fact that some people *do* like us, despite the roadblocks we put up, should be enough to make us step back a minute and think. But if these feelings are harbored for too long of a time, they become a limiting belief and, if not addressed, will begin to form the emerging personality. After years or even decades of continued existence, not only have we forgotten why we feel the way we do, we also become addicted to the emotions of these beliefs, making them even harder to shed. We then organize our lives so thoroughly around what we believe, we don't even know we have issues. This is a messy problem to solve!

Meditation

This seems to be a good place to introduce the practice of meditation as the primary ride of choice for our soul journey. At this point in my travels, I had dipped my toes into the meditation game and had been experimenting for a little while. Meditation refers to the act of "going within" to find answers to deep personal questions on spirituality and why our lives are the way they are. Prayer and contemplation are other modes that can get us there, but we must be careful for there are distinctions. Meditation places the seeker in the driver's seat. We note we have a problem, so we ask for guidance to understand. We also ask for signs to show us a way out of them. It is implied that when we get those answers that we act on them! Prayer, on the other hand, is asking God to deliver Divine help. There is no real directive to come up with your own personal plan. This is how I learned prayer as a child. As a matter of fact, we were even given the exact words to say! When I prayed, I just "hoped" I would be heard. When I meditate, I know I will be given an answer that advises me what to do. In meditation, I feel like God's co-creator. In prayer, I feel rather like a lost soul with little control of the outcome. This, of course, is my personal experience. There are others who have wonderful experiences with prayer and/or contemplation.

I have certainly known about meditation for a long time. I was never, ever attracted to it. I also had a completely different personality a couple of decades ago, so I was not ready to make this kind of commitment. When I started to learn about the magic of our lives and our universe, I realized I needed to know so much more about myself than I did. Meditation provided the path, but it wasn't easy.

There are so many different types and styles of meditation. Some forms require a lifetime of practice. Many forms are for very specific purposes. Much of this information was way over my head. I decided to take baby steps and purchased some short (twenty-minute) guided meditations. I didn't have to "do" anything except follow the instructions and relax. Just like anything else, meditation is a skill to be developed. It takes time to learn to quiet one's mind so that we can hear ourselves. It takes some discipline and focus to train our brain so we can discern the messages inside. It is a lot of work, but the benefits are immediate.

It wasn't more than a month or so that I just started feeling physically better. Aches and pains that plagued me throughout the day seemed to have minimized. The emotional swings I always went through in a day were diminished. I noticed this, and so did others! It was encouraging, and it allowed me to stay on my path.

Over time, I found guided meditations distracting. When I discovered that I could manifest and heal myself, I wrote my own program. I had taken on manifestation and was specifically creating a new future for myself. That involved a lot of detail and a lot of imagination. I had goals. I saw myself as a writer. I saw myself living somewhere else. I saw myself as a person filled with love and compassion and *forgiveness*. The idea of forgiveness was new to my game, but it soon became evident that I had a *lot* of forgiving to do, and that included myself! I also meditated on some of the difficult topics I had been learning while writing this book. Some things were confusing, and I needed clarification. Meditation had become my laboratory.

Mindfulness is important for meditation, not only while we are meditating, but also afterward because many of our answers come later. We don't want to miss them.

There is a reason that the subject of mindfulness has become such a hot topic of late. There are mindfulness schools, mindfulness studies, mindfulness attitudes, and more. The big emphasis on mindfulness highlights the importance of *paying attention and being aware* of everything we do throughout the day, regardless of its significance to us. Remember, we are observing all day long. This means that everything we see is a possibility that we can bring to life in a unique way. When we are mindful, we are living in the NOW moment. Why is this important? Because it is in the NOW moment that we can hear messages from the spiritual realm and from deep inside our subconscious. It is in the NOW moment that our intuition bubbles to the surface, and for a tiny second, we know our purpose. It is from the NOW moment that we will experience visions and a deep connection to Source if that is our aim. It is only in the NOW moment when all other distractions are quieted down enough that we can hear this soft, quiet guidance and finally swell with understanding of a mysterious truth. These voices are quite soft. We need to teach ourselves how to listen. If you are thinking about the past or the future, you are not in the NOW. NOW means now! [6] [7]

Perhaps my greatest meditation discovery was what I learned about unconditional self-love. Because of the history of my past, I had no love for myself. I knew this and knew it had to be addressed. A good chunk of my time was working with my child-self in meditation. I sought to comfort and love that child . . . with no conditions! This took months. As I noticed I was becoming more "whole," I also noticed I was losing my fear of rejection. I was losing the constant evaluation of how I was stacking up. I didn't worry about being considered a fool. Honestly, it didn't matter anymore. If I messed up, I would laugh and move on. End of story.

This has been my greatest miracle and greatest gift! I think Patrick reached this stage, too, toward the end of his life. But what I learned will live with me forever. You simply can't love anyone enough if you don't have yourself front and center as the most important recipient of the great love we all have to share. Our ability to love others is exactly matched to the level of love we have for ourselves. We can do nothing until we start with self first!

Conclusion

As a convert to a new concept of divine creation, I now realize how important this work is and how grand. Each one of us resides in the midst of constant creation. We should consider ourselves true artists and our product a unique and one-of-a-kind result. Going about such creative activity in a multi-tasking, ho-hum, "needs to get done" approach certainly doesn't give creation the respect it deserves. Now that I know so much more, I approach my creative efforts with greater understanding, more humility, a great deal more respect, and much reverence.

Further, when I now embark on producing anything new and different in myself, I make sure to acknowledge all those on the other side who are working furiously to answer my new vision, which I know wouldn't be possible without them. It's important to render a high level of appreciation for what is being done for us. It truly pays to be grateful!

CHAPTER SIX

The Truth of Free Will

Heavenly Hindsight

SOURCE, IN THE PROCESS of creating life eons ago, had many, many wonderful gifts available to present to his creations. He certainly didn't have to give us any gifts at all, but he loves us, so he did. It is interesting that the one Godly gift he selected for us, out of an infinite number of others, was free will.

Why is this more important than patience or compassion or just a general benevolence? Because, in his Divine wisdom, God knows that free will, if used properly, is the key to unlocking access to *all* of his other gifts and attributes, including patience, compassion, and benevolence. Why hand out the goodies piecemeal when we can have access to all of it? He wants us to have it all because of his great love for us. He also knows that winning these wondrous attributes lies in the struggle to reach them and take them.

We stand before a door that we know protects all the wonders of the universe. The door is closed to us. Without a key, we could never have to a chance to enter and explore this treasure chest of the Divine. Free will is that key. With it, we gain access to this sacred realm and can pick and choose anything we want and do anything we want to do.

There is only one caveat . . . In order for us to get past just a viewing of the treasures within and actually select exactly what we want, we must choose the right gift for the right reason. God left us to our own discretions to decide what that would be. This is when it pays to heed the saying, "Be careful what you wish for."

All choice is sacred, for its effects reach far beyond ourselves. There is nothing that we do in this universe that doesn't affect everyone and everything else.

Using our free will to make the right choice for the right reason means that it will benefit us individually as well as collectively, and it's all for the Higher Good.

Because free will is a gift, we own it forever. We will always have it. We can never lose it. God will never take it back. Oh, we can ignore it for a lifetime or two, or we can misuse it, but we will never have it taken away for any reason. It is our safety net, our way to redemption and eternal happiness. When you reach the other side, you will realize how much power we really had available to us while incarnate on earth and which we never accessed or used appropriately. You might just kick yourself!

Free will is intimately connected to creation. We know we are driven to create. This is as natural and automatic in the corporal world as breathing is. We don't think much about the gift of breath much, do we, as we meander our way on earth? We take it for granted, until we encounter a situation where it is compromised, and then we appreciate it! It's the same with free will. It is so natural to have it, we just don't think about it.

When we are in the human form, we are always looking for shortcuts . . . an easier way to get things done. Unfortunately, we have done this with free will. We decide to ignore the condition that our free will dictates making the right choice for the higher good and . . . just skip the higher-good part. We have been happily making self-serving decisions without concern for others for a long time. This isn't true to the meaning of free will. This is simply just free choice, which is free will's ugly cousin. Free choice does not give any power to creation. It can manifest nothing. It is simply doing what we want, when we want.

When we use our free will, we decide to join the universe of the Divine and, as a result, have access to all the power and miracles that live in that space. As long as others can experience the joy and love we produce when we choose wisely, the sky's the limit.

When my parents decided that I would invest six weeks of my life in yet another rehab program, I really felt that they had taken away my free will. I felt that they forced me to do something I would have never chosen for myself. In reality, all they took away from me was my free choice, which was akin to taking away a favorite toy. My free will, which I had put on ice for most of my high school years, wasn't even visible for the taking.

Free will is a big gift, and it is to be used for big things ... such as creating. My creating days were few and far between at that time. When I learned I would be making this diversion, my "true" free will leaped to the front and center of my consciousness. I felt threatened by the decision. I held hope that my free will would emerge to help save the day.

I just didn't know what I was going to do with it. My parents' proposal offered other choices to make ... move out, get a job, join the army. I had the power to go that way, but I didn't. At the deepest level, I realized that the life I would create if I took a different path would not be the best choice for me. I would not be happy or fulfilled. Instead, I chose the option offered because, in my heart, I knew the promise of a better life might be more possible. I would have a fresh chance to create something new. It took a great effort of will to decide to go along. It was the decision of a lifetime!

There was something else going on that I wasn't privy to at the time. I would be leaving the earthly plane in nine months' time. I came to earth with a purpose and lessons to learn. Where on the path to accomplishing any of this was I? I was only eighteen years old. Would this be enough time?

The rehab program in which I participated was called Wilderness Quest. From my perch here on the other side, I call it Soul Quest. For not only was it a program to deal with the earthly lesson of addiction, it was a program that served to rehab my soul as well. My story is chronicled in the journals and workbooks we were required to keep. I have kept them in their original form because those on earth who read them will be able to relate both to the subtle and grand changes that occurred. I had more than just an addiction to drugs to work on in this life. There were other lessons as well.

What a tidy remedy I created for myself! By making the right choice, I covered everything I needed to learn in this lifetime ... everything!

The Truth of Free Will

The decision to use our free will is the very first step we take in the creation process. The decision to make a change is an act of creation itself. We already know how hard-wired we are to creation, whether we feel it or not. All we know is, even if we feel we have everything we want, if we stop creating, we feel an "agitation" because we have ceased to create. Creation is the food for our souls. It is a powerful life-giving force! We must feed our hearts and soul a steady diet of change, and free will is the necessary appetizer.

Free will is one of the most underestimated aspects of our humanness. We toss it aside as if it's neither here nor there. We were born with it. We have always had it. We will never lose it. Yet we rarely think about it, appreciate it, or recognize it for the wonders it brings. Needless to say, because of our carelessness in putting attention on it, we have neglected to uncover its true power and thereby benefit from what it can really help us accomplish.

There is no real science behind free will because it is part and parcel of who and what we are. I compare its existence to how we feel about the body package we live in. It's how we come here to live. It's what we are used to. We accept it simply as the way things are and what we have to work with while we are here. We know we have it, but because its application is natural, we don't think about it much. We don't think to appreciate it.

Since we are also here to learn lessons, it is solely through our efforts at creating a different way to see the world or our own personal situation that we can discover the truth of that lesson and how it applies to us individually. Creation is how we learn to grow and understand. In the process, the lessons we are sent here to learn will reveal themselves in a way that is different than what we are used to. Seeing our challenges in a new context leads to understanding them at the deepest level. What this means, then, is that the choices we make when we decide to create *have* to be elevated ones. They *must* be the right choices for the right reasons! [1]

What is Free Will?

Free will is not just the right to make a choice . . . it is the *right* to make the *right* choice. It differs from *free choice*, which is getting to do whatever we want whenever we want. Free choice is an earthly aspect, not a Divine one, and attaches no heavenly condition. Executing the *right* choice under free will is heavily implied. The distinction is important. [2]

> *"Will is very strong in the incarnate human. They need to have a lot of power because the human body is a perpetual motion machine that requires willpower (at the most basic level) to operate."*
>
> —G. Stoller [3]

At the very least, we make the choice every single day to stay alive. This is so automatic that we aren't even aware of it. Think about how many conscious choices we make every single day using our free will.

You choose to get up in the morning to go to work, even though you don't want to. You choose to make that trip to the gym . . . even though you don't want to. We use our free will so often and so regularly that we have forgotten how powerful and grand this gift really is. It has been relegated to a lower tier of gifts received. We have given it little glory in the scheme of things.

I think most of us can tell the difference between choices that will significantly affect our lives and those that might provide simple and usually immediate gratification. If we truly understand how enormously we can change our lives by deciding to create something new in it, why aren't we doing this every single day?

Unleashing the full power of free will and selecting the correct choice requires a great deal of attention and thought. Even if we do know the difference, we already own free will and never have to worry about losing it, so what's the rush? We'll get back to creating a more meaningful life another day. Deep inside, we know that when we are ready we can dredge up the power of our will and use it to create something grand someday. Right now, it's just too much work.

But when we decide, really decide to reinvent ourselves and our lives, we will have access to a lot of supernatural help from those benevolent entities on the other side who want to see us succeed. This is indeed good news! Since the decision to change is actually an act of creation itself, we attract nothing but beneficial energy to us. When we finally offer our plan to the Divine in the proper frequencies (elevated emotions), we will be heard! Once the message is received, the divine universe, including our angels and guides, begins to work immediately on the messages you are sending. They are now creating . . . on your behalf! How do you know this is happening? Watch for the signs of synchronicity and coincidence!!

Free Will and Limiting Beliefs

Just like everything else in our lives, despite our right to possess this God-given gift, our ability to use it can also be compromised by limiting beliefs. I offer a pretty good example of my own life where I believe I gave up the power of free will for a time because of some early limiting beliefs.

As a young person, I was not always sure I would be taken care of properly. The chaos of my youth created moments where I found myself on my own and didn't have the maturity or wherewithal to know what to do about it. There was more than one occasion where, in my effort to "fix" things, I got myself into a pickle . . . a big pickle! When I think about these situations today, I shudder at the dangers I now know lurked nearby. I also think how it was that I got myself out of these situations and realize that, in every single case, my salvation had nothing to do with anything I personally did. Rather, some extraordinary circumstance occurred, leading to a direction of safety. In some cases, an earthly "angel" appeared out of nowhere to save me. Major coincidences that probably saved my life seemed to randomly come together in just the nick of time. This is a great example of a special kind of help I mentioned earlier from those on the other side whose sole responsibility is to protect us. (This is the job Archangels do . . . protect us from harm that is *not* in our plan.) I was in the face of great physical harm in the situations mentioned above. How they resolved was truly miraculous.

These experiences had a profound effect on me. I sensed I needed to create some sort of safety net for myself that could keep me out of trouble. So I started to plan my life around what I wanted to do and had to do and made a schedule to fit it all in. The plan promised comfort and safety. I wanted to know what to expect. I never wanted to be in danger again. This worked for a long time.

Up until recently, I realized I had planned my life around appointments, schedules, to-do lists, time, and anything else that might look like stability. Stability has always given me much comfort. When I have a place to go every day, when I know what it is I will be doing every day, and when I know my day will be filled up with activities, I feel "full." I belong somewhere. I am part of things. Because I have chosen each and every thing I will be doing, I know I will be safe. I know what the outcomes would be and (mostly) what the effect will be on others. My schedule is my comfort.

It was so comfortable, in fact, that I stopped creating. I stopped working on myself because I was now safe and secure. I was also very unhappy. The early limiting belief I erected as a child was a stable life was a safe and happy life. As an adult, I became addicted to schedules. There was little time to create. But we live in a universe of constant change! So our lives are going to change whether we expect it to or not. There is no amount of scheduling or planning that will accommodate the death of a child. This kind of change never figures into our plan. Change, however, is critical to the creative effort, and the decision to change is a genuine act of free will.

Why do we walk away from a treasure chest of gifts and abundance when we can have anything we want? Fear. Fear of the unknown. Fear of change. Fear of the ability to live a different life. Fear of success and the changes that come with it. There are so many fears that paralyze our will to grow. Most of them can be attributed to limiting beliefs, either about our self-confidence to do something different and grand or about our opinions (judgment) of the kind of life we find ourselves attracted to. For some of us, an inventory of the limiting beliefs we are holding might be in order before we start working on the grand plan. We need to clean house first.

Using our will to make creative choices uses a lot of energy! Visualizing and mindfulness need to be on full alert and active before it is "all systems go." The process will take time, sometimes a lot of time. Our free will is at work the entire way deciding on this or that and revising this or that prior to implementation. This effort is not for the faint of heart.

It is for the full of heart.

Giving Away Our Power

Though the plan was always to be masters of ourselves, somehow we lost our way. We have given away much of our power to others who claim to know what is best for us. Further, we have submitted ourselves to a form of "mind control" by allowing images from television, movies, magazines, etc., to inform us of "how" we should be. This invisible control has particularly affected western society. We have been so distracted!

Over the millennia, as we evolved societies to make our existence on earth a little easier, we gave up some of our free will by choosing to live in communities that we established to take over some of the decision making and labor requirements previously executed on our own. This, of course, was for the benefit of the community, which was important to us for our safety and growth, especially as the world grew bigger. Somehow, however, over many thousands of years, the sacrifice of the individual will to that of a group of others has resulted in competition, rivalry, division, war, anger, and fear, among other states. As a result, many of us feel helpless today because we have forgotten that we have the power to change the situation. Over time, it seems we have not only forgotten we have free will, we have forgotten how to use it.

Today, the external circumstances of our existence are so out of balance that our very survival feels threatened. We are experiencing major climate changes and shifts. Sea levels are rising. The skies are heavily polluted. There are over seven billion of us on this planet, and we live here as if the natural environment will never change. We really weren't aware, until relatively recently, how much damage has been done. Something has gone horribly wrong. Now we worry! We must reclaim our rights and our power!

This is a good time to bring up one other aspect of free will.

There have been many instances in historical and present times where our right to free will has been physically violated.

> *"When you can't control what is happening, challenge yourself how to respond to what's happening. That's where your true power is."*

—UpliftConnect.com

False imprisonment, fear of death, torture, etc. are situations most of us don't volunteer for. All is true here, but authentic free will refers, as well, to the choice to carry a benevolent "attitude" regarding the things that might happen to us. There is always the bigger picture. There are things we can't see from our limited perspective. If you would like an excellent example of the power a positive attitude can bring to a horrific life, read Victor Frankl's *Man's Search For Meaning*. [4] Involuntarily imprisoned in a Nazi concentration camp, Frankl used his skills as a psychiatrist to determine that those prisoners who survived the experience carried with them an attitude of acceptance but filled their minds with wonderful thoughts of loved ones day in and day out. This created *meaning in their lives* despite the current circumstance. These folks tended to survive! This was such an inspiring story! When I apply this to my life and seem to be faced with circumstances that I feel are "outside my control," I am learning to use my will to imagine other reasons, possibilities, and outcomes than the one that just plopped itself down in front of me. Is there an alternative way to think about things?

At the end of the day, however, we have a gift, and we are obligated to use it. We are *obligated* to make choices in our lives. We are here to learn and grow. It is only through our choices that we can grow and evolve our souls and consciousness to the next level. When we feel free to fully engage the power of our free will in order to create, it is so fulfilling to see our plan shape and grow. Later, when there is feedback from others that our work has touched them in some way, the sense of validation is powerful and expansive. Trust yourself. No one can create like you. The world deserves to see it! Use your will to make things happen.

The Masks of Free Will:
Free Will, Free Choice, and Errors of Non-Choice

"Choice is the most powerful thing on earth. It is the recognition of the difference between want and need that is causing events to be so out of balance."

—G. Stoller [5]

A broader discussion of the individual will and the collective will is handled inside Patrick's journal. I offer a touch more on free choice. Related to free will, free choice is just the freedom to choose without assessing benefit to any other person or experience. It is just doing what we want to do . . . good or bad. There is little purpose other than self-gratification. Free will, on the other hand, should be loaded with meaning if we use the gift in a benevolent way. Free will captures our attention because we know, if we use it, we *will* change. From the viewpoint of the Divine, however, our motivation to use our free will to benefit others as well as ourselves will earn us the right, as cocreators with Source, to access that Divine treasure chest that holds our most noble dreams.

Free will is the access path to Divine and deliberate creation.

I have never attributed my failures in life to lack of will, but perhaps I should have. If I want something, I just go after it . . . if I want it. There have been other times I have been keenly interested in something but chose to let it go due to lack of confidence or some other limiting belief. In hindsight, I have made errors of non-choice that have held me back. Not making a choice is also a choice. Still,

I never attributed such actions to a "misuse" of free will. Taking the gift for granted and not holding it sacred is a clear misuse. By not making a choice, I am missing out on the complete freedom to express myself in the best possible way. Could any of the choices I bypassed earlier because of my insecurities attracted new and wondrous opportunities to my life? What could I have created and contributed? I know the answer is a big yes . . . had I known then what I know now. This is the regret some of us have experienced when we make an error of non-choice.

On Death

There was one more unexpected idea I came across regarding free will, and this one should interest most of us. When we have completed our plan here on earth and are "complete," we can then *choose to die.* Yes, *we* choose when we die. Part of this is covered before we arrive here, and we pre-select the life we will lead because we decided it was the best life to learn a particular lesson. Part of this includes our death plan. The only time we may change our pre-planned "death" is if we use our free will to do so. We may have discovered a "higher road" to follow that can affect the outcome or we may get distracted and follow a less-lighted path. Nothing is set in stone until we make the final decision and act on it.

Throughout our entire existence on earth, however, we have the free will to live by the plan we chose before we arrived here or we can abandon it altogether. Of course, that doesn't change the fact that whatever lesson we are here to learn will not have to be learned at another time or in a different way. We are absolutely responsible for taking care of our business one way or another.

If we have lived our plan, however, and are happy with our contribution, we will be ready to move on. We come here to do what we need to do. It's not necessary to stick around, unless of course your free will comes up with another good reason to stay . . . in which case, I imagine we might live longer than the original plan.

This power of choice is mighty indeed. Having said that, it is amazing most of us are still so fearful of death. In death, the only thing that dies is our corporal body. *We, our consciousness, as energy, will never die.* We have lived so many lives before this one that it's really sort of silly to fear death. Unless we know we have reached absolute perfection and don't need to incarnate anymore, we'll be back.

> *"Just as we are all born at the perfect moment, there is a perfect moment for us to leave earth. You can leave when you're ill or you can leave when you are complete. We aren't really meant to die from pain and disease. This choice is available to all of us."*
>
> —Soqyal Rinpoche, *The Tibetan Book of Dying and Living*

Honestly, we have gone through this so many times, we should know the drill by now. Make the choice not to fear death. It is a good fear to lose since, if death is inevitable anyway, fearing it will not change the outcome. Death is simply energy that is changing from one form to another. Of course, this isn't news to the divine universe, but if this helps at all, there is certainly a lot of celebration when we do finally leave this earthly plane and return home!

Making Change

I found it terrifying to give up my cornerstones of safety for something new. Yet it seems I was being led to this very act. I was very addicted to the "stable state." I was also extremely unhappy with my life. It took some time, but I finally convinced myself to just do it. I looked for other ways, trust me. I would have to change.

Perhaps if I viewed my efforts as creations vs. "making changes," it would have put me in a healthier state of mind. When I think of creation, I think of something shiny and sparkling and new. When I think of making changes, I think of repairing some imperfect aspect of myself. I might even be mad at myself for having let things get out of control. In this case, I am certainly not seeing myself as that perfect being that God sees. All I see are my flaws. With creation, all I see is beauty. To finally make the decision to change took a huge amount of willpower. It was not comfortable, largely because of the pervasive fear I had of change. Fortunately for me, my unhappiness was unsustainable. I was feeling its effects both physically and emotionally. I had to choose to face my fear of change in order to see myself as shiny, sparkling, and new. I would have to choose a journey into the unknown instead.

> *"Everything you do right now ripples out and affects everyone. Your posture can shine your heart or transmit anxiety. Your breath can radiate love or muddy the room in depression. Your glance can awaken joy. Your words can inspire freedom. Your every act can open hearts and minds."*
>
> —David Deida, 16Personalities.com

The last thing to remember about free will is that its use requires energy. Anything we do with our free will requires energy to manifest. Energy never dies. Energy changes matter. When we activate our willpower, change happens whether we are aware of it or not. We on earth expect these reactions to follow a linear course, naturally. Certainly this is true when we apply free choice to our menu. When we use our will, however, to make the right choice, the effect on others operates more like the stone that creates ripples in the water much further away from the source of initial impact. Using our will stretches well beyond our immediate vicinity. Believe it or not, this applies to the little decisions as well as the big ones. Energy affects all in its path. Energy is always in motion. One act committed by one person can impact far more people and situations than we believe. Our free will can truly be a powerful tool when appropriately applied.

The Journal: Wilderness Quest

I was excited the day I was to leave for Utah. I love to travel! I hadn't travelled much in my short life but did get in a couple of family trips to Hawaii. I had plans to do a lot more, so this was an adventure. Mom, Dad, and my sister took me to the airport, and after goodbye kisses and hugs, I was on my way. When I arrived in Salt Lake City, I was directed to a special bus that would take me to Moab, Utah, a good three hours away.

Once we got out of Salt Lake City and the bus was on its way, I was dumbstruck by the beauty of the desert and the red mountains and incredibly blue sky. It was turning to dusk, and that night, as I was gazing out of the bus window, I saw the most beautiful, huge red moon I had ever seen. For the first time in my life, I was speechless. I was so excited over this incredible display of nature that I called home.

Breathlessly, I was describing the view to Mom. Whatever worry she may have harbored at that time disappeared. I think my reaction made Mom happy. She was hopeful. I was hopeful. Hopeful for what, I wasn't sure, but hopeful nevertheless. I was beginning to look forward to this journey.

It was late at night when I arrived in Moab, Utah. The bus dropped me off in front of the rehab office, an old complex of cheap buildings surrounding a concrete courtyard. I was met by a greeter who ushered me into a sleeping room. I was told I would be taken to my group in the morning and needed to be ready by five a.m.

The next morning, I was given a backpack, bed roll, some tools, a workbook, an academic workbook, and a journal. A driver met me in an ATV and drove me through the woods and onto the mountain. This was truly beautiful country. I had very little to say, as the beauty overwhelmed me. I also had no idea what to expect and knew I would get no answers if I asked. I enjoyed the silent journey.

When I reached camp, my group was out on one of many, many, many day hikes I would come to know later on. A counselor remained and spent the time going over the workbooks, expectations, and rules with me. I took the day to familiarize myself with the contents.

The Personal Success Workbook would be the official chronology of my recovery. After an introductory section on graduation requirements, dress code, conservation practices, safety instruction, the Circle and Community Law, the book delved into the issues of addiction. The workbook was separated into chapters based on AA (Alcoholics Anonymous) strategy with corresponding soul work for each step.

There were inspiring stories, explanations, and descriptions of certain behaviors that I would be personally addressing. After each area of discussion, we had to respond to a myriad of questions about our own behavior. It was hard to see how all this would help me, but I dutifully completed each and every assignment. Over time I started to see patterns of behavior and "stink'in think'in."

The academic workbook was a handy little gem with all the primitive survival skills I would need to endure my time out here. The particular quest program I was enrolled in was also very high on environmental and earth science awareness. Every effort was made never to leave signs of human-ness in these mountains, forests, and woods. It was strictly minimal-impact camping. Specific dangers of this particular terrain, such as slick rock, stream-bottom hazards, dangerous cliff rims, sand dunes, scary plants, insects, animals, and weather were covered. Further, we had hard skills we needed to accomplish by the end. These included making a spoon out of natural materials, a dig-throw, finding material for cordage, making fire, using a map and compass, making and setting traps, and learning to tie all different kinds of knots and discern what situations they should be used for.

The journal would reflect my daily activities, thoughts, dreams, fears, and hope. We had to write every day.

My living arrangements included living with a group of one or two counselors, six or so young adults, both sexes, and involved satisfying our individual requirements and learning to relate to others in close proximity. We were expected to participate in an AA-defined "Circle" every day, and we were expected to be *honest*. There it is! My first major challenge.

There would be a lot of hiking! Every day, in fact. But in addition to this, there were special hikes in which we were expected to participate. Several solo hikes were on the agenda in addition to an independent walkabout and a group walkabout. These were all-night hikes, which usually covered about twenty-five miles, and other hikes shorter in length, but treacherously dangerous. Rappelling and other skills were required to tackle these.

Further, we were charged with finding our own water and hiking to a food resupply area, which always changed, once a week. There was little discussion about bathing and laundry. That's because it was catch as catch can. If there was time and there was a stream nearby, we might be able to take care of those little hygiene items.

Of course, all of this was just words on paper at the time. I had no idea what to really expect. Even though I had never been truly alone for any part of my short life, nor had a wilderness experience, nor had gone a day without a bath . . . well, except maybe when I was ten and would stick my head under the shower to "prove" to my mom that I bathed . . . I was looking forward to this new adventure. I was particularly interested in the hikes.

6-20-2002: Moon 5 Hands High (P.M.)

Three days out in the field and they already put me on a solo mission. Your fears rear their ugly heads when you are alone. I just realized today how long this program is going to be. It freaked me out for a little bit. But then, good ole AA came to me: ONE DAY AT A TIME! It helps make your goals easier . . . you take on today without dreading about the future.

After tonight I will have a day and a half left on solo. I am looking forward to the hikes afterward. I still haven't gotten my feet wet yet. Hopefully, the altitude won't give me too much trouble. Well, I can't really see anymore and this pencil is getting dull. Till tomorrow.

6-21-2002: 3 Hands High (A.M)

Yesterday (after my first solo), when all of the other students finished night hike, I felt a little twang of jealousy. Ramon (counselor), wouldn't let me go on night hike because it was only my third day out in the field. I don't really blame him because I haven't even adjusted fully to the altitude yet . . . somewhere around eight thousand feet. I can get a little tired just hiking to a water source and back. Despite this, I wish I could have felt what the others felt after completing a twenty-nine-mile hike in the dark. I got to help drop glow-sticks instead.

It's okay, though, my time during solo will help me adjust to this altitude, and I have some tough hikes to look forward to. I will have my time in the limelight.

5 Hands High (A.M.)

I am reading a copy of Narcotics Anonymous and discovered something that struck me as very relevant and true: "We can no longer blame people, places, and things for our addiction." This one really makes me think, mainly because I am out here alone doing just that. All of my fears, anxiety, and feelings have to be dealt with. Not by the hand of anyone else . . . just me. I am responsible for making my life better . . .

Reading further, the element of this book that stands out the most is the strong emphasis on finding God. For some reason, this is very difficult for me. I know that if I turn my life over to God, I will have reached a state of utmost serenity. I think that this is one of the roots of my problem. I do not wish to surrender. I know I am powerless, but I struggle with the spiritual aspects of "giving myself to God."

7 Hands High (P.M)

My, what an eventful day this has turned out to be! No one ever said solo had to be boring. Out of nowhere, it started to pour down raining. This is pretty ironic because even the staff chuckled about us getting rain out here in the summer desert. As I hurried about to get my stuff covered up, I uncovered an ant about this big {--------}. To my disdain, it scurried right into my sleeping bag! There was nothing I could do since it really started to come down hard now. I hopped in the sack with the little bug and covered us up with my blanket. Eventually, the rain stopped, the sun came out, and my little ant friend got relocated to a nice home deep beneath the sand.

Reflection

The quiet. The quiet. Until I got on that mountain, I had never really been alone. It's a different experience to be with yourself and only yourself. The absence of noise in addition to one's first aloneness only highlights a strange and new experience. When there is no noise, you think, you reflect. I was wise not to do too much thinking on my first day out. Instead, I read NA to beat the boredom. (We were only allowed certain reading material.) Because it was so quiet, the words I read resonated loudly. With no interruptions, no distractions, no man-made noise, the words I read were beautiful. It was as if I had read them for the first time. I also reflected on the fact that being in nature felt like I had come home! It felt right to be here. I knew I could find my heart here.

When I got to the section on God, I was rattled. My parents raised me Catholic, but really the church offered little benefit to my family. My dad grew up under a non-denominational faith, and my mom had a strong bend to spiritualism and the metaphysical, despite her Catholic upbringing. I had no real relationship with God at all in my life. To surrender to someone or something I didn't know didn't make sense. But I also believed in something much greater than myself, so knew I would have to take this time here to find God and get to know him. Maybe then, I could surrender.

Nevertheless, it was the quiet at the end of the day that had the greatest impact on my first solo experience. It occurred to me at the time that this was probably what meditation would feel like. Only in the case of meditation, most people "go inside" purposefully. Since I hadn't been around long enough to discover this wonderful tool, I learned how to do the same in the silence on the mountain. As a matter of fact, all of our hikes were, in fact, a form of walking meditation. Our solo was to be done in silence. Our independent walkabout was a twenty-five-mile night hike with no sleeping and no talking. It's amazing how things are so much clearer from my current particular viewpoint.

The Circle

I was glad my first experiences in this program were hiking, walkabouts, and learning a few survival skills. The next experiences would be far more difficult . . . dealing with people. At least once a day, Circle was held. Up until this point, my partner in healing was nature and quiet reflection. But I was living with a group of people that I had to interact with, get along with, and survive with. I couldn't be aloof anymore. In Circle, this group of "broken souls," including me, would be my healers, my friends, and my mentors.

Since I entered the world of the user in my youth, the relationships I had with those I thought I cared about were using relationships. I used drugs in order to fit in, to not feel different from others, but to create friends. I did not like having to sacrifice my morals to do things they thought were cool, but I did it because I didn't know any other way to attract people. I loved work, but I hated the internal conflicts. When this happened, I would either fuel the disagreement or do nothing to put an end to it. I hated the social aspects of high school . . . cliques, groups, politics. I liked being around girls if they were using, but I had no intention of attaching myself to anyone.

In those rare moments during rehab when I decided to commit to changing my ways, I would do well . . . after much effort. When the waters cleared, however, I would relax and fall back to "home base," and this was when complacency set in. When I got complacent, I used! The guilt associated with this had devastating effects on my self-esteem. I would use, think I was no good and believed no one wanted to be around me. Then I would isolate, and the drama would start again. I blamed others. When I was questioned on my activities by friends or others, I would blame them for their intrusive questions. This extended to blaming the whole world where I believed everyone was better than me and I was nothing.

Circle was the place where I would learn what honesty was all about. Circle was the place where I had to share my thoughts and feelings. This was a terrifying prospect for a professional liar who isolated to cope. I wasn't concerned about Circle at first. After all, I had spent nine months in AA and peer group counseling, so I did have an idea how to interact in a crowd. But the Circle in this program offered no hiding places. I couldn't put on that "slick," cool persona with this group. It was unsustainable as my group was getting to know me too well. It happens when you spend 24/7 with the same group of people for six weeks in an isolated wilderness area. This was going to be rough!

Anyone can call Circle. Anything can be said in Circle. The activities of the day are discussed and feelings shared regarding those activities. Any emotions or personal experiences are also discussed. It was a place to deal with conflicts, frustration, and sharing both good and bad impressions. Most times, the Circle was organized around the twelve steps that make up the AA program. There were Circle rules to follow as well as the camping rules.

6.23.2002

I got off solo today. We had a very long circle afterward. It was very emotional for Elena. I think we all got something good out of it. I talked about how I read the NA book and how it will affect my life in the future.

Reflection

I was rattled after Elena's time in Circle. Such pain! Such sorrow! To hear this expressed with such honesty and feeling was soul shattering for me. This was nothing like rehab or AA meetings! This was gut-wrenching distress, and for the first time, I felt enormous empathy for another human being. I listened and felt. I didn't know if I would ever be able to share in this way. I left Circle with a confusing array of new emotions and a sense that there are others out there who are dealing with way more challenging things than I ever had to deal with. But, in the wisdom of the Circle, all pain is equal. Something minor to me could be major to someone else. Pain is equal in its application. It just hurts. A small kernel of appreciation for some of the advantages I had been given in this life were taking root and seeping in between the seams.

6.25.2002

Ohhhh, man. Early this morning we had resupply for our food. It added about ten to fifteen pounds to our packs. After Circle we all started off on a predicted nine- to ten-mile hike to Monty's Flat. It was very hot, our packs were very heavy, and I was pushing myself very hard. While we were on the ATV trail, the hike was going well. Marcus was leading it and kept a very fast pace. We took more belays as a group than I thought we should have, but I appreciated them all once we got to the steep access. We huffed it up that for about half a mile and then had to hike another two-and-a-half to three miles to camp. The last few miles were *murder* for me! My muscles felt like they could go no further and I couldn't wait to get to camp. Once we got there, I was utterly amazed by the view. You could see about a hundred miles of beautiful canyons. It was a very hard day, but the view was definitely worth it!

Reflection

I wish we had stayed on that mountain with its beautiful views of the canyons. The next day, we had to hike down into the valley and camp. While beautiful from a distance, our camping area was overrun with cows, cow dung, grass, and bugs! The day was interesting. I was going to lead Circle with Elena that night, and we got a new student whose name was Adrian.

6.26.2002

The meeting was very good. It felt good to lead and be at a meeting. It was a great experience. I realized how much I missed going to meetings at home. I also realize how much I miss my family.

Reflection

It had been one week since I entered this program. It was also about this time that I had what I considered to be my first major breakthrough. I was trying new things, new ways to communicate and behave . . . of course, the rules on behavior kept me in check. But the combination of nature and the very close living arrangements with my group of people created a perfect recipe for eventual success. All of the ingredients I needed to change myself and my future were at my fingertips, albeit in a highly controlled environment.

My Journey to Understand: The Collective Will

In reading Patrick's journal up to this point, I sense the interplay between how he wants to be and that which his "group" is trying to get him to see. His experiences in Circle were very emotional! This was a huge breakthrough. While I know he felt them, Patrick displayed little emotion, other than anger and surliness, before his rehab experiences. There were times when I saw him "pleased" about something, but I rarely saw any evidence of compassion or empathy. Because the first rehab was on an outpatient basis, I sensed his attention to his attitude in therapy was left at the therapy office before he came home. I noticed little changes, but nothing too transforming. When I read how emotional he was during Elena's time in Circle, however, I was surprised. It must have been a very powerful session to evoke such a reaction.

The Collective Will

There are two levels of free will on earth: the individual will and the collective will. On earth, the collective is the sum of all human souls on this planet. Both levels are necessary for our personal transformation. As a matter of fact, when we keep hearing our efforts must benefit the higher good as well as ourselves, the higher good piece refers to the effects we have on the collective. We can't do this work alone. Later, we will learn about connection and the divine relationship we have to all of God's children. Connection is the last thread that holds it all together, for when the collective will is on the same page as the individual will, we have just "hired" billions of souls to boost our personal exertions along. Now imagine how *right* you would feel about your chosen path if the entire world were in agreement and supportive of your choices. Can you feel the energy that might produce? You probably would feel like you could do anything!

Our collective will, however, is as withered from misuse as our individual one. But it is awakening! The effort starts with the individual will. For example, we personally notice that the area we have lived in for a couple of decades doesn't look or feel the same. Weather catastrophes, dirty air, too much traffic, and cranky people seem to all have changed and not in a good way. We worry. Perhaps we are consuming too much; perhaps people just don't care. We may not do anything about it because we don't know what to do. Where do we start? Then, somehow, we learn that there are millions more who are feeling the same way. (Another great example of like attracts like!) Our energies are being matched by similar feelings of others. Somehow this energy synchronizes into a message of "Something Needs to Change!" When this happens, physical events come together so that the "collective message" can be heard. We are seeing this today through BLM protests and the intense attention on child abuse through sex rings, kidnapping, and slavery. How can we think we are the only ones thinking the thoughts we have? Expand that vision and find others that share it. This is how the collective works, and when the collective awakens its true power, miracles happen.

We do not have to accept the dictates of those who have taken away our power. In past times, when a collective of intention tried to change the status quo, there were many martyrs for the cause. It was a traumatic time to live in, but with persistent effort, our situation did indeed change. It couldn't have happened without that groundswell of energetic emotion from the citizens of earth. Really, most of us aren't that far apart in how we would like to see our world. We yearn to live in freedom, nonjudgment, compassion, noncompetition, and cooperation. All of this is for the taking when we act together, when we pray together, and when we support each other in our individual efforts. [6]

This is the reason we must never work in isolation toward our higher goals. We must pay attention to the effect on others as we build our dream. Remember the story of the artist in *Seth Speaks*? When others can see themselves in our work, we will attract nothing but abundance to our efforts. It's as simple as that.

In the past, the instinct of the collective was to survive cataclysmic events. It's been a long time since we have suffered through the destruction of our inhabitants through deluges, earthquakes, disappearing continents, collisions with comets, and so much more. Today we need to wake up! The application of the collective will has done nothing but collect mothballs. The situation in the world today has changed things. We are angry. We have been taken advantage of. We are suffering. Slowly but surely, these nudges are attracting our attention. We *are* waking up, but we need to move a little faster.

Patrick was challenged in his Circle. He could see his counterparts participating in a truly authentic way. In this case, it was the *influence* of his small "collective" in the wilderness that pushed him onto a path of true recovery, and that would involve honesty. Just as an individual thought can influence the reaction of others, a *collective* thought can influence the individual. The energy of his group was pushing Patrick into a new direction. This is not easy to fight against. I'm so glad he hopped on and "went with the flow."

The Journal

6.27.2002

I got to know the new student pretty well today. Adrian is about twenty-three years old, and I think he is serious about his recovery. Very cool guy. The hike was very dull today. It was a shorter hike … getting ready for the big one tomorrow. The camp we are at is called Bow-Hunter. I'm not very thrilled about it. There are millions of red ants that live under the pine needles we are sleeping on. Our group had a great AA meeting today. I am really enjoying them and look forward to more in the future.

6.28.2002

Last night I got to share my personal life story to the group. I think it went very well. I got some great feedback. Some people questioned if I was willing to give up everything for my recovery. I honestly do not know. I feel that I have a safety factor when dealing with people that prevents me from becoming extremely emotional. It was probably for this reason that my life story sounded a lot like "regurgitating facts." I really want to work on this area of my life, and I want to share this with the group.

Reflection

I was, indeed, changing. At first, when we did Circle, I would try to change my image by pretending to be someone else. The key word here is "pretending." That was just another form of a lie. There is a huge difference between pretending to be someone else and changing into a new person. I was jumping ahead. The result wasn't particularly satisfying since I really hadn't done the work yet to be a new person. Feedback from my Circle group validated that there is no shortcut available for this effort. I had to do the work.

Because of my behavior, my self-esteem was shot. I blamed the world. Everyone was better than me. I was nothing. I used drugs to create a new me, one that would cause others to like me. The results, obviously, were devastating. The more I used, the worse I felt. Then I would isolate. Every time this happened, my self-esteem tumbled even further.

I valued others' approval over my own. I agreed with others, compromising my values so they would like me. I did not drink after emotional disappointments, from pressure or stress. My using did not affect work. I did not drink after my friends were done drinking. I did not have any physical symptoms from drinking (i.e. shakes or needing a drink in the morning). I didn't ever feel that it would be impossible to live without drugs. I never panicked at the thought of running out.

I gravitated to friends who I felt needed me, thereby lessening any fear of rejection. I spent a good amount of time creating a character that I believed would be accepted. There were so many different versions of me that I had a very difficult time setting boundaries with my acquaintances. Friend requests, coworker requests, my own work addictions all created more anxiety over the fear of being rejected. My mantra was "I will try to make people like me anyway I can." In order to maintain this charade, I felt safe by keeping feelings to myself and working hard to please others. I did not trust others. I feared disapproval and rejection.

I also knew, even though I ignored it personally, that this was a path to nowhere. Actually, it was a path to something . . . more unhappiness and more self-defeating "stink'in think'in." In our Personal Success Workbook, there was a short poem by Portia Nelson called "Autobiography in Five Short Chapters" that helped me see where I was at this stage of my life.

Autobiography in Five Short Chapters
By Portia Nelson

I. I walk down the street. There is a deep hole in the sidewalk. I fall in. I lost. I am helpless. It isn't my fault. It takes me forever to find a way out.

II. I walk down the same street. There is a deep hole in the sidewalk. I pretend I don't see it. I fall in again. I can't believe I'm in the same place. But this isn't my fault! It still takes me a long time to get out.

III. I walk down the same street. There is a deep hole in the sidewalk. I see it is there. I fall in . . . it's a habit. My eyes are open, I know where I am. I get out immediately.

IV. I walk down the same street. There is a deep hole in the sidewalk. I walk around it.

V. I walk down another street.

I was at Chapter II.

6.29.2002

A lot of drama happening for me and my program. Well, not really, but I have made big steps toward recovery. Last night Ramon (counselor) was over to have Circle with us. He told us a story that I could really relate to. It had to do with honesty and integrity. I had to decide if I could relate to what the masses do or what the one honest person will do. Sadly, I related to the masses. I shared that in group and started to get a little emotional about it. I told the group how I thought that I was a part of the masses and how that relates to my future college experience. It will be hard not to use! I got lots of good feedback. I have determined that if I am going to have a sober college experience that I will need AA in the background. I have risked and put much more of myself on the line. It feels good.

I led the group on the hike today. I was very happy with how it went. I got us there quickly and efficiently even though we had a few roadblocks (i.e. following a bearing straight into a canyon). The reason that I volunteered to lead was to take a step up in the program. I took myself out of my head and onto this ground.

We also spotted mountain lion tracks, bobcat tracks, and found a huge horny toad lizard really close to camp.

6.30.2002

We had a mini layover day today. The staff had to go to a meeting, so they left us at our campsite all day. It was a very productive day for me. I did some laundry, wiped off the dirt on my body, worked on powerlessness (from my Personal Success Workbook), and completed assignments in my academic workbook.

The atmosphere here is very silly. Everyone is just kind of hanging around being themselves. I really like talking to Adrian. He and I sorta clicked, and we can really relate to each other. I hope he stays in the group till I leave.

Tomorrow is supposed to be one hell of a hike. I am on Day 6 of no anger outbursts and Day 5 of no swearing. I hope I can make it through tomorrow's hike without messing them up.

7.1.2002

Good day today!

It is the first of the month, and it's also resupply day! Not to mention, the hike kicked ass because we did a huge vertical access where we had to hold on to roots and shrub oak to keep from falling. We had another surprise waiting for us when we got to camp . . . FRESH MEAL!!!

Yes, today is a very good day. The icing on the cake was Larry (Head of W.Q.) came by last night and told us we would be summitting a mountain that no human has been on for years!

I've been talking to Adrian about it, and he agrees that today is a very good day.

Reflection

Slowly but surely, I was getting strong. I was acclimating to the altitude, the exertion, nature, and the people. I was doing my workbook and really making an effort to be real in Circle. The personal workbook helped a lot toward helping me to untangle the motivations, behaviors, and emotions that ultimately led me to this place. Having to do Circle everyday made it difficult to create a personality and maintain it. It was just a hell of a lot easier to be real. I didn't have to remember so many things to keep up whatever the façade of the day was. I felt so much more peaceful. I would discover much later that Circle would be the place where the miracle of change would occur for me.

My physical strength was off the charts compared to when I first arrived as a sickly looking, thin, tired young man with red-rimmed eyes. I was hauling ass on these hikes and feeling the benefits. My new love of nature took on a world of its own. It was nice to look at the world with awe and wonder again. All this in just under two weeks!

7.02.2002

It feels like Christmas morning! The hike today had tons of goodies to get. I now have a completed fire set, yucca for cordage, two new-looking rocks, tinder, and more. We had a great downhill access, but we had to then bushwhack our way through a thick wash for about two miles to camp.

I was a little frustrated . . . but then I made fire! Sage on sage, I am the man!

7.04.2002

Today's hike sucked. We camped in the middle of the wash last night, and we resumed bushwhacking at about eleven thirty this morning. (I know that because Kristen told us.) It was a very long hike and took over five hours to go three miles. Hopefully, tomorrow's hike will be easier and shorter because we didn't get much accomplished in our Personal Success Workbooks or for our program other than the hike. How frustrating.

Reflection

What a difference a day makes! Finding natural supplies for survival is an empowering activity. The earth gives us everything we need.

We take and sometimes we give back, but mostly we take. I am learning a profound respect for nature and its infinite genius to provide for itself and its critters, including man. I am learning that nature will do what it needs to do. It has its own special wisdom. Just like giving me the gifts that I needed to make my tools. I am learning gratitude for these gifts.

I am also learning I can't control outcomes. Just like on the second day when bushwhacking took up most of our time. I imagine patience will be the next thing I learn, since I was so irritated I couldn't work in my PSW. This feels like it could have been a good situation to just "let go." If I had, I wouldn't have been so irritated with the bushwhacking. Eventually it got done, so what was the rush?! I feel I am returning to the natural order of things, including the right time for the right thing in the right place.

I also noticed how disappointed I was that we couldn't do Circle that second day. Feeling disappointed for missing out on an opportunity to be my authentic self?? Now there's a shift! That prospect, back in the old days, would have me running for the hills. I also think I'm starting to like this guy named Patrick. It's nice to see him again.

7.5.2002

Well, so much for that. Today's hike was about twice as hard as yesterday's, and we didn't even do any bushwhacking. We all woke up very early and hiked up a very steep access to get out of the wash. Our goal for the next two days is to hike to the base of Mt. Linnaeus today and then hike up to the summit in the morning.

After we hiked out of the access, we realized that getting to the base of Linnaeus was no easy task. In fact, that was due to the fact that getting to the base meant we had to summit an adjoining mountain. In other words, we had another four to four-and-a-half miles of *gradual* uphill to go. About eighty percent of the way through, the counselors thought we were at our destination. The only problem was that they did not know where the water was.

They sent Adrian and me down a very steep access in order to search it out. We found two small streams after hiking over an hour on our own. When we hiked back up, the counselors decided that it was not safe and that we should hike to another location forty-plus minutes away where there was water "for sure." By this point, Adrian and I had been hiking most of the day and it was about five p.m.

We were all getting pissed off at the staff because they couldn't seem to get their shit together. By the time we got to the other campsite, we were all exhausted and frustrated. Staff wanted to have a Circle to discuss the "us vs. them" attitude on the hike. Then they searched for water for over an hour. When they found it, we discovered it was actually a smaller water source than the one Adrian and I found earlier.

After I got some water, I came back to camp and saw that Ryan had given up trying to make fire. (It was his night in the rotation.) Kristen was trying to make it instead but wasn't having any luck. Sooooooooo, I pulled out my sage kit that I had collected a few days earlier. I made fire before our counselors did (and in the dark, I might add). I got to be hero for the night!

After dinner, I stood out on the ledge of our campsite and looked down on the lights of the city of Blanding. It was a beautiful view, and all in all, the day didn't turn out that bad for me.

Reflection

Despite how this day started, it turned out well. I think I just got an idea that the challenges we are faced with, both big and small, eventually pass on. At the time they present themselves, it feels like doom and gloom—in other words, the end of the world. But they pass, their time comes and goes. When they present, I feel like they are offering me a lesson to be learned. Since they won't be here that long, it's best to learn in the time they are offered. Because guess what? They will return to finish the job and will keep returning until we get it. Oh, and the delay might cause the lessons to be more difficult. Might as well get it done when it needs to be done and save myself some time. I must have done something right this day as I felt I was rewarded with the ability to make fire for my tribe.

7.06.2002

We basically had a layover day today. Most of us slept in until we woke up naturally. I did the same. It was nice to relax and hang out and have a lax day until our "hike." I was extremely pleasantly surprised when Kristen told us we were climbing from 10,800 feet (our campsite) to 10,900 feet (the summit of Mt Linnaeus). We had basically summitted the mountain yesterday. It only took us about fifteen minutes to climb the last hundred feet.

Though it was a short hike, the view was considerably amazing! The vast lands below us were easily the coolest scene of nature any of us have seen yet. I got some great pictures. Hopefully, the ghetto Walmart camera they gave us will take quality photos.

Buried at the base of a boulder on top of a lookout point overlooking the canyon was a time capsule with a notebook in it for everyone who has summitted the peak to sign and write a few words. That was cool to do.

After we had Circle on the top of the mountain, we came down, and I busted a coal for lunch. That's right, I got signed off on fire!! We had a late dinner a few hours after we had a meeting. I went to bed with a full stomach and feeling very content. ☺

Reflection

The Mt. Linnaeus excursion was life changing for me. I don't know … this spot felt sacred, holy. It was truly a God-like experience to see how incredibly awe-inspiring and *large* and majestic nature really is. I felt so small, yet at the same time, I felt so much a part of what I was seeing and experiencing. I could be wrong, but I think I was beginning to understand just a little bit of what it might feel like to find God.

My time capsule quote said, "There is only one problem with life ... no background music!"

7.7.2002

I offered to lead today's hike. It was kind of crazy because I didn't really shoot a bearing or anything. Kristen kind of told me where to go and I did. I wonder if I will get signed off on map + compass with this hike. I pretty much randomly led the group through some scary woods until I hit a trail and followed it to camp.

After a short nap, four kids (including me) tried to bust fire for dinner. I ended up busting it first. That felt good. After that, we had a really good AA meeting. I definitely can't wait to go to more when I get back. It is getting pretty dark, and I am just rambling on, so I will call it a night.

7.08.2002

Today is our official layover day. I had a hard time sleeping last night because I was thinking about my family and Team Xbox. They keep us completely cut off out here, so I can only hope everything is going well and that everyone is okay. I miss home very much. I hope this feeling passes because it is torture.

Anyway, I am completely out of food right now except for some powdered milk and corn meal. Today is our resupply day so I won't have to wait too long to get some more food in my system. It's funny. On lazy days like this, I realize how much of our time out here revolves around food. When we aren't hiking or discussing things in Circle, we are eating in between. As a matter of fact, I'm hungry right now.

Speaking of that, Ramon is supposed to come out to our group today. He was gone for a week at some conference and told us he would come out the following Monday. He also might have a surprise for us . . . *slaughter*! That's right, we might get to kill and eat our own food today. Hopefully, he won't let us down . . . W.Q. is known for that.

Anyway, I started to read *Lord of the Flies* today. It's a good book and eats up some of my idle time.

7.09.2002

Well, we didn't get to do slaughter yesterday, but we had a very good Circle. When it was my turn on the hot seat, I discovered and verbalized to the group that I have trouble showing my true emotions. I would rather tell people what they want to hear than give away my hand of cards. I also discovered that I tend to run with the people that feel the same way I do about things. Tonight in Circle I am going to try and break out of this pattern of behavior. I truly hated the hike today. Instead of telling the group that I had a good day, I will tell them how frustrated I was.

Little by little, I will break out of my shell . . .

Anyway, despite the shittiness of the hike, there were some funny parts.

Out of nowhere, we had to climb down this extremely steep access with loose rocks. There was one area where it was way too steep to climb down with our packs on. So we had to toss our packs over the edge and hope they caught on a bush or something. Mine snagged a little tree and was hanging there by one canteen. I scrambled down the access and was about to grab my pack when I heard Ryan yell, "Look out, Pat!" He had thrown his pack down behind me. Of course, his bedroll collided into mine, and they both went head over heels all the way down the access. They must have been rolling at full speed for a good thirty seconds. All of us could not stop laughing. When we got to where the packs were, Ryan's was way busted and mine wasn't. Ironic. Funny shit!

We just had Circle. I felt that I had the best share of my life here. I felt so real! It was awesome. I just want to remember this feeling. I want to keep it and remember how the others reacted to me. I feel so real now!

Reflection

The combination of disappointment (no slaughter), exhaustion (obvious reasons), and the really gnarly, ugly hike cracked something inside. That, plus the bout of homesickness the night before, just shook something loose today. Suddenly, I wanted to change. I wanted to be whole. I wanted to be real. I made a sincere commitment to make that change happen in Circle. I decided to talk about those emotions. And the result? The Best Circle Ever!! I truly didn't know what it felt like to be me. I had so many personas in my life, most of them fabricated. But to be me and be loved for it? This was something well beyond my normal perception of reality. And this is where I wanted to be all the time. It truly was a breakthrough.

By finally deciding to change, I emotionally embraced the idea that I could be a new person. I felt the power I had in myself to make myself my own hero. In my case, I was desperate to just be real! When I took the risk and opened my heart in Circle, the outpouring of love, support, and compassion was overwhelming. I had never had such an experience before. It was one I promised myself I would repeat over and over again. In doing so, I began the process of changing myself at the cellular level.

7.10.2002

Today has been a good day. My goal today in Circle was to stay positive during the hike, and I am happy to say that I accomplished it. The hike was tough, but I had fun with it. Chris, Marcus, and I led the rest and smashed through the wash all of the way to the pack trail. We were all then eaten alive by a swarm of *killer biting flies*! It was insane. We moved ourselves over to the nice flat, clear trail to camp. Adrian and I set up a shelter and just ate with the rest of the group. I'm extremely tired and can barely keep my eyes open. I just have to remember that I need to keep my feelings open to the group!

Now, I'm gonna take a nap . . .

7.11.2002

Interesting day today. I had a very good sleep last night, and before I went to bed, I volunteered to lead today's hike. It definitely kicked ass! We had about two miles of gradual uphill to go on the pack trail we were on yesterday. I hoofed it up as fast as I could and left the group in the dust for a while. Once they all caught up with me, I shot a bearing from a main road perpendicular to the pack trail to camp. I got us to our location about thirty minutes from that point, and we were there before noon. MONEY. $$$.

We actually ended up at the exact same campsite we were at a little over a week ago. The one right before we hit that downward access into the wash.

The reason this day is interesting is because Larry came to visit our group and introduced us all to the new Executive Director of W.Q. They both sat down and were talking to us for a while, and out of nowhere, Larry looks to me and asked, "So where are you with your recovery?" Major hot seat! I got pretty uncomfortable and rambled on about a few things and finally said, "I do not want to use anymore." That was good enough for Larry. After he moved on, I realized that I really don't want to use anymore. I want to have a good relationship with my parents, and I want to have a future. Using is not in the equation.

Reflection

It's official. My breakthrough was complete!

7.12.2002

We had a pretty emotional/confrontational Circle last night. The staff told us they were pissed off because they felt that there were no group dynamics. I definitely see where they are coming from.

Reflection

Yeah, I spend most of my free time with Adrian or Marcus. While I get along with the others, I have to say I'm not really invested in their situations to the extent I can be useful. This, I believe, is a pattern I have played out my whole life. I haven't been active in solving problems in a group situation. I always found work conflicts unsavory and stepped aside letting others fix it . . . or I added to the conflict (for sport) . . . just for the heck of it.

There really is no excuse for this out here. We are a small group. Our success and our survival depend on how well we work together as a tribe. That involves more than just finding water, food, or making fire. I realize I need to connect to the energy of this particular community. If we all did this with an open heart, I think we would all be much happier and content. This type of positivity benefits the whole as well as the individual. I thought perhaps I was well on my way to full recovery. It seems I will have to dig a little deeper.

7.13.2002

I got cut off yesterday. Out of nowhere, we had a surprise Circle with special guests, Larry and Ramon. When Larry came to our group a couple days ago, he "sensed" that our group did not have a strong enough drive for sobriety. So last night he told us we were going on a "Group X" hike. Our expedition would be solely our responsibility, and staff would not join us. He gave us two maps and points of location to plot on them.

Right now, I am writing from our first campsite. We hauled ass today. It's going to be a nice relaxing day without the weird and *annoying* staff. We are going to try and haul ass again tomorrow and get to our "Sobriety Destination" a day early. We are headed for Deadman's Point . . . irony, anyone?

Also, in the Circle last night, Ramon really pissed me off. He told me that I was going to Family Meeting when the others in my group go. Despite the fact that I started a little late, he then said I was nowhere even close to being ready and that he thinks I am blowing smoke up everyone's ass. BULLSHIT. He comes and talks to us once a week . . . if that . . . and can determine whether or not I want to be sober?! I don't think so. He doesn't even talk to us on an individual level. I really do plan on being sober when I get out of here, and I am worried that he is the one blowing smoke up my parents' ass. I am serious about my future and my sobriety and above all the relationship I have with my parents.

I want to make up for lost time, and I want my parents to know the real me.

Reflection

The final challenge! The last ingredient to the soup of recovery I was cooking. Ramon didn't know how serious I was about my sobriety, and this challenge was a test of my resolve. It made me angry. Now in the past I used anger to further isolate myself and continue to do just what I wanted. I never physically lashed out at anyone, and my verbal utterances were usually confined to a couple of under-the-breath sarcastic comments. This time I used my anger to "prove" myself to Ramon and the powers that be. I wanted them to *see* the change. There was, however, one more challenge coming . . . proving myself to *myself*!

7.15.2002

I skipped a day of writing because our hike yesterday was *long* and *tough*! Ryan woke me up at first light and asked if I could help wake the others up so we could get off to an early start. I was fine with that until I looked over a few minutes later and Ryan was back in his sleeping bag. Hmmm . . . something's not right with this kid.

Eventually we all woke up and took off on the day's hike. Our goal was to make it to our Sobriety Destination by nightfall. We had an access, a pack trail, and miles of road in front of us. The access wasn't too bad, but it took us a little while to search for the pack trail. By this time, the temperature was up to about ninety-six degrees. We thought that we had it made once we hit the pack trail, but I guess we overlooked the fact that the trail elevated over a thousand feet in about one mile. What a fucking climb! Thanks to Larry on that one.

After we "summitted" the trail, we had about three miles to our third water destination . . . all on roads. It was pretty flat, and we made really good time. We unrolled and ate and refilled our canteen to prepare for the next three miles to camp. Some of us (including me) tried to sleep but were attacked by flies and couldn't. We washed our socks down in the stream instead.

Once we were all rerolled, we started on our last stretch as the sun was going down. Once we were about three quarters of a mile from camp, we stopped at a huge clearing. After talking it over, we decided to stay there so we could stargaze and avoid the extremely annoying trail staff, who would probably be waiting for us.

This morning we all had little to no food left, and we were extremely hungry. We got up early and hiked the last three quarters of a mile to camp where we were hoping to see our resupply and water. There was only water. That sucks! There was a note that said we were to wait at this location until Ramon and the trail staff came to prepare us for night hike.

I am sitting here eating raw dough waiting for Ramon to bring us our food so we can eat before the hike. It's going to be a LOOOOOONG night . . .

7.17.2002

Man, do I feel good today or what?! Yesterday morning I completed night hike!! I left at nine forty-five p.m. and arrived at camp at five forty-five a.m. Eight hours!! Eight hours of hiking! At night! They never tell us how far we went, but I am assuming it was about twenty-two miles. They sent me off second, after Marcus. They kept a half-hour increment between students. I ended up passing Marcus less than halfway through the hike and finished thirty minutes ahead of him. That means I closed a thirty-minute gap and added a thirty-minute gap! I kicked ass on that hike. Ramon said I was an animal. My average speed was about two-and-a-half to three miles per hour. Not bad considering I only stopped once.

We all had Circle after the hike with Ramon, and I feel like I have made a ton of progress. I now feel that I have an accurate bearing of what it is I need to work on to insure my sobriety.

The Circle was very good. When it was my turn to check in, I told Ramon and everyone else the truth. I told them that I was tired. All of my exhaustion has weakened my defenses and I can let true emotion through. Earlier in the Circle, Ramon told Bryan that his parents did not know what to do with him. Ramon repeated it three times to make sure that it sunk in his head. For some reason, that hit me very emotionally, and I felt like crying. It scares me to know that I was not that far away from such a situation.

That is my reality. It is also in my reality that I can still lose my parents and my family if I choose to pick up drugs again. I need to realize that I am never in a safe place. I must always keep my guard up.

For me to do this, I need to be <u>true to myself</u>. I have spent so many years lying to myself and hiding from myself and my true emotions that it has become second nature for me to live outside of my reality. I can't do this any longer. I need to open up the flood gates and feel.

Reflection

Mission Accomplished! It took a twenty-two-mile solo night hike over eight hours with just me to impress myself. I was finally getting the hang of the "proper order of things." First, love God. Next, love self.

My emotional reaction to the discussion of Bryan's parents was the first authentic emotional response I could remember in a very long time. For weeks I was trying to create a new me. It was hard, but heavy physical activity broke down my defenses and made the effort bearable. When I had that emotional reaction at Circle, I felt a massive shift from the inside out. I was opened. I sought solace from my group. I had compassion for Bryan's parents. It all happened at once. I felt whole. I impressed myself and was beginning the process of self-love.

7.17.2002 (continued)

Right now I am on solo and have until 7/18. This also means that I have gotten all of my solo mail from my family. God, I have missed them all <u>so much</u>!! I can't express how good it feels to hear from them finally. It has truly re-energized me. I received seven letters, five from my mom, one from my dad, and one from my sister. It is great to get clued in on all of the hometown news. But more importantly, I have discovered that my parents (mainly my mom) want to work on opening the lines of communication with me. Almost <u>exactly</u> what I thought we needed to work on without even having looked at their letters yet. It feels so good to know that I will have their support in this. I feel that the Family Gathering will be key in orchestrating a successful future for all of us.

I feel so good right now! Only six more days until Family, and I have ants in my pants (literally!) and can't wait to see them all.

I was also wrong about Ramon before. He is pretty good at determining who is serious and who is not. I can learn a lot from him, so I need to keep my ears open.

Right now I am sitting in the middle of one of the craziest storms I have ever witnessed in my life. There are tremendously dark clouds above me, and hail is dropping in buckets. The thunder is so loud it shakes the ground.

Wow, that was amazing. I can't believe my shelter held up to that. The whole time I was singing:

"It's raining,
It's pouring,
The old man is snoring,
He woke in bed
And bumped his head
And couldn't get up
In the morning!"

That was pretty intense. I got some pictures . . . hopefully they come out. Now I never want to go through that again.

7.25.2002

I've been neglecting my journal lately. After I got taken off solo, I have been preparing for the dreaded event . . . Family Circle. We hiked about a mile away from our solo location to a really nice spring. We had a layover there for three days until we were to be picked up for Family and driven to Monticello.

Reflection

This was it! Finally, Family Circle. The prior four weeks, including all of the self-discovery work, nature work, roughing it work, and group "therapy" work, had been leading up to this very special event.

After a three-day layover, which included rest, food, Circle, role playing, and preparation in our workbooks for Family, the group was ready. Family was where it all culminated. This was where the rubber met the road.

I don't think my family has any idea what they are in for. I didn't either until we had a chance to role play and discuss the individual, highly personal, and gut-wrenching topics we would need to bring up. This was to be done in a community setting with my tribe and all our family members present. The group is to bear witness to what we learned, how we have changed (or not), and listen to our plans for the future.

Oh yes, Circle was the beginning, the turning point, or the end. I was nervous and at the same time exhilarated. I was awash with emotion. The excitement of seeing my family again, the anticipation of wondering how they would react to the process, and the nervousness associated with wanting them to see how much I had changed, how much I love them, and how much I wanted them to be proud of me vibrated in every cell of my body.

My Journey to Understand

A Clash of Wills

While Patrick may have felt that his free will was taken away from him when the Wilderness Quest option was presented to him, it was obvious this was not the case. We offered several alternatives . . . army, move out, etc. If he didn't like these, he was free to come up with one of his own.

The only option he couldn't choose was to stay home and continue his behavior. That would have tread on *our* free will to live our lives the way we envisioned. By the way, when this "threat" was presented, we had no intention of changing our minds. I personally was prepared to let him go and do his thing, even if it wasn't for his highest good. This was my "surrender." I did not have the power to change him, but I didn't have to sit around and watch his personal destruction.

Free will is with us twenty-four hours a day, seven days a week. If you think about it, we are faced with some sort of choice just about every minute of every day. Sometimes the task at hand is small and insignificant, and sometimes the choices we make using our will are massive and transformative. When I read Patrick's journal, I see the struggle with his will through his words. He so wants to fit in and be admired and do the right thing. The training program, however, he put himself through in the past to please others emphasized an inefficient approach. The changes he sought were cosmetic, surface changes. None of them were tasked with helping him find his true self. Nearly eighteen years of lying and pretending and creating some persona he thought was cool and that would attract friends had failed miserably.

These activities really were the result of free choice, not free will. It takes free will to get beyond the fear of discovering yourself. It takes a lot of *attention* to activate your free will in this way. It takes free will to actually find out who you really are.

The journey can be scary and difficult. Somehow, in the past, we came to believe certain negative things about ourselves that had nothing to do with the truth. Why we latch on to this negativity is beyond me. Now, I am talking about myself. In reading Patrick's growth through his journals, I can see how this transformation is a series of tiny baby steps to the truth. It is a process that begins with a new thought, a new possibility, and the courage to try it out in little and benign ways.

By "being trapped" in a drug rehab wilderness program, Patrick finally had the opportunity to find himself in silence, with the help of nature and the support of his tiny community on the mountain. There really wasn't anything else to do, so he just did it . . . probably because it was easier than resistance.

Either way, I could see the effort each day as he wrote in his journal. Every day, something new challenged him, and he took the time to *think* about it. He questioned himself, his friends, and his counselors. He was weighing the effects in a positive and open way. This was a side to my son that I had never, ever seen before. Reading his words brought nothing but joy to my heart. Hearing an honest testimony as to how he felt about all this, both good and bad, was a wonderful revelation.

In order to survive, Patrick had to pay attention to every challenge that was placed in front of him. Most of these challenges, especially the "nature" ones, arose from situations with which he had no knowledge or experience. In nature, you *have* to pay attention. Things can go wrong very quickly. One needs to stay alert. With each act of insecurity that we push through, however, we change. The practice with nature prepared him, I believe, for the tougher work of dealing with people in an honest way. He seemed to jump in wholeheartedly.

In the course of this work, I also noted that he was actually starting to really like himself! Now this is something I completely relate to. Being a "self-hater" myself for as long as I was, I found I was experiencing his joy as if it were my own as he started to love himself again. It gave me the courage to continue with my own work because, well, I just *really* like that feeling!!

I used to think Patrick didn't have a heart. After hearing his story, I saw how truly large his beautiful heart was. This was the gem he was shining up! My own heart swelled in response.

CHAPTER SEVEN

The Truth of Connection

Heavenly Hindsight

WHEN WE LIVE ON earth, we feel so alone. It's an attribute of the very dense energy that is indigenous to this particular environment. Because we can't see it or hear it or touch it, we don't believe we should be feeling any other way. It doesn't take much to train oneself to search for the signs that we are all connected to each other in some way, but some souls never even try. The reward is a lifetime of loneliness.

In true fact, we are deeply connected. Those of us who live here in the LBL know this intimately. Granted, it is a lot easier to experience deep connection in a world where communication occurs through not just thought, but instantaneous thought! I am perfectly tuned to all the entities that exist where I am now. So much so that anything I decide to do creates an instant attraction of spiritual volunteers to help me do it. The love generated from Source and the rest of his creations is so intertwined that each purpose becomes the purpose of all. God's purpose becomes our purpose. There is no disagreement that one thing is more important than another. Each soul holds a sacred place when "The Body" is involved. There is a great deal of power in connection. It is the same on earth.

Fortunately things here are organized in such a way that we can break things down a bit to work on the detail of whatever we are planning. Within the quantum field, there are groups of souls that have been together throughout many, many earth lifetimes. These groupings are not random in the least. Families, best friends, mentors, and others who are at a similar level of soul development exist for the sole purpose of helping each other in their quests for perfection and oneness with God.

Mentioned earlier, everyone in a soul group works on everyone else's earth plan. So many minds helping just one soul! That's how much love there is for our single, individual life! The beautiful news is that everyone's life can be worked on simultaneously. No one gets left out!

A soul group can consist of anywhere from five to twenty-five souls. This is the primary group, and these souls will reincarnate with each other in different roles played out from lifetime to lifetime. It just depends on the lessons one chooses to learn.

All souls are completely unique and have a set of talents, abilities, and gifts that can be perfect to help a soulmate attain understanding. The level of importance a soul plays in the earthly realm depends on the healing gifts they bring to the table. In some lifetimes, they play a major role and in others a minor one. It just depends on the objective. Of course, the human form a soulmate takes when they become incarnate depends on the specific role they agree to play. Some lessons are better learned when they are delivered by the right person with the right look. All of this is considered.

Our soul groups aren't the only souls that help us throughout our earthly residency. There are other major and minor players from other soul groups who have just the right energy to lend a hand. They may appear once or twice in our lifetime and make a tremendous impact on our progress and journey. This might be the teacher, the mentor, the lover, or a homeless sage who appear with some message or other gift that reminds us why we are here.

Further, there are angels, who are not members of a soul group, and who appear to protect us from danger and any other situation that may prematurely cut our time here short. There are our own personal spirit guides and/or master guides who are *always* with us. They inspire, send messages in dreams, visions, or feelings, and keep us on track. Many of these elevated souls have been with us for as long as our consciousness has existed.

Until I arrived at this heavenly place, I had no idea how much help we are getting! If you could see the activity and energy from my place, you would be awed and amazed. You certainly would never imagine how you could have possibly felt so lonely!

As a soul group member, my life on earth was a very successful one. From this story alone, it's obvious I had a lot of helpers on earth working with me on my plan.

After my physical death, my soul was elevated to the level of Teacher. This is definitely a promotion! Now, because soul group members tend to advance in the divine field *together*, it is one of my jobs to make sure the other members of my group advance with me. Those members who are a little behind are going to get a little extra help.

This is part of the plan. We are so connected that it's best if soul groups advance together, so as not to disrupt the universal tapestry under construction. It's all part of God's plan. There are occasions when one member advances quite rapidly. In this case, adjustments are made, but for the most part, we stick together.

For all souls, elevated or not, connection is the lifeline to God that holds us all together. God's will is strong. The connection will never be broken . . . ever. God *is* the connection, and he is going nowhere anytime soon! All will wait until every entity reaches its ultimate purpose . . . the final connection to God.

When we finally see ourselves in all others and when we bridge the connection to them through our creations, we are truly operating in and for the divine plan. Once this occurs, we can then combine our powers to create massive change for the greater good, for humanity, and for our precious earth.

The next part of my story demonstrates the power of connection. I had reached the final stage of my earthly life when I participated in the Wilderness Quest program. The last thing I needed to learn was the power of connection.

The story that follows highlights the strength of community both in my recovery phase and in my post-recovery phase. Without this experience, I would not have had an understanding that everything I did affected others . . . and ultimately myself. I would also not have understood how strong the common will can be when it decides to focus. There is no fighting against this if you are the only one.

The Truth of Connection

As I continued to uncover answers to all of my questions, the one that kept niggling was that of my demeanor after Patrick died. It bears repeating that the overwhelming emotion I experienced was gratitude. *Gratitude!* How incredibly odd. I was grateful, though. I was grateful that I had my real son back. I was grateful that Patrick was so happy and pleased with his new self. I was grateful that, for once in my life, I had made some really good decisions about the venues for his recovery. I was grateful for the college experience (yet to come) and the friendships he made there. I was proud of him. I felt fulfilled. At the time, all of these emotions felt completely natural when Patrick was alive. It just didn't seem to make sense for them to persist after he died.

It wasn't until I started to delve into Patrick's life that I finally found the answer. It wasn't until I learned that the lessons we might have carried with us from a past life into the current life could be removed from our karma tray *and* our current life when we finally recognize the lesson in front of us, know what it means, and clear it. It also wasn't until I learned this truth of connection and put the puzzle pieces together that I realized I had cleared some significant karmic debt by participating in the Family Circle described in the journal section of this chapter.

> *"We think of ourselves as autonomous individuals making our own decisions and leading our own lives. In reality, we are a matrix of connection. We are connected to each other through our neural networks and by means of invisible energy fields . . . our thoughts and emotions are* not *contained within our minds and bodies. They affect those around us, often without their knowledge."*
>
> —D. Church [1]

Family Circle

Family Circle was the culminating event of the Wilderness Quest program. This was where all the discovery work done on the mountain, all of the revelations that came out in the daily Circle meetings in camp, and all of the input and effects of living with a small group in the wilderness for six weeks came together. The participants were now ready to face their parents and families with an honest appraisal of their past, what they'd learned, and how they saw their future. Family Circle was a "witnessing" event where everyone involved, including the extended families, could view the truth of transformation in their child, brother, or sister.

> *"There is much sacred energy in the gathering of the group. There are no strangers, no separateness. No one stands alone."*
>
> —B. Weiss [2]

Everything was put on the table during those three days in Family, not just by our family, but the others. The experience was soul wrenching, painful, joyful, and cleansing. All of us cleaned the slate of everything, good and bad, that had gone on before. We were honest in our self-assessments and completely forgiving of all indiscretions. We forgave ourselves and each other. Our compassion and empathy for the other families peaked to super-high levels. This was one of the most powerful connections I have ever made to any group in my life. It was raw but powerful. For me, the experience was an epiphany! Despite the fact that we were strangers to each other, all the families were bound together by a common problem . . . love for our children and compassion for the others that have also suffered so much pain. Unbeknownst to me at the time, all of the "soul work" the families had to prepare prior to Circle and the actual sharing of it in Circle was a massive effort designed to clear "debt" with each other. For the participants, an honest accounting was necessary. Honesty and forgiveness from the families was also expected.

What about that grateful, peaceful demeanor at the funeral and beyond? I believe because I had cleaned the slate with my son, I would be spared deep, debilitating grief. *This* was my reward and gift for having the courage to face the lessons I needed to learn and clearing them once and for all. When we learn a lesson, we don't have to suffer anymore. None of this would have been possible if it weren't for the connection to a community of strangers who supported me and my family in love for three days. I continue to remain enormously grateful. I was also healed.

The Invisible Thread

An invisible thread connects
Those who are destined to meet
Regardless of the time, place, or circumstances.
The thread may stretch or tangle,

But it will never break.
May you be open to each thread
That comes into your life—
The golden ones and the coarse ones.
And may you weave them
Into a brilliant and beautiful life.

—**Chinese Proverb**

Signs of Connection

Have you ever experienced a poke in the ribs that came out of nowhere and made you jump a foot? And then, for some strange reason, you think of your dad who passed? In the twilight hours of dawn's sleep, have you ever woken up to a kiss on the cheek and immediately recognized it as the touch of a friend who recently died? Have you heard a voice in your head that wasn't your voice? Have you ever felt a loving warmth envelope you and you have no idea of the source, but you think of your grandma? These are not figments of our imagination, just figments of life on the other side and a promise of help and hope. When we speak of connection in the Divine realm, we aren't just talking about humans on earth. We are including all those who have lived before. We sometimes forget to include these souls in our grand plan, mainly because of our 3D life and the fact we can't see or touch them, but they are there! Connection applies to the spiritual worlds as well as the physical ones. Why should we be concerned? Because all souls are doing the same thing . . . connecting to their place in the tapestry . . . even those that are gone. It is these heavenly counterparts, however, who will be there for us, giving Divine messages of love and assistance, signs and synchronicities that our plan is working! I, personally, *need* this kind of feedback. It is validating and comforting. It is also just fun to come across those synchronicities. They are always so surprising.

Still, when we choose to take this journey, it is, indeed, a lonely undertaking. As we work quietly in prayer or meditation to deal with our negative emotions and learn to love ourselves and others more purely, we are doing this work . . . alone. It is easy to forget that every time we pray or meditate or perform a beneficial act, we are positively affecting everyone around us. (Remember the ripple effect?) Of course, this is an energetic effect, so we don't see it right away. Sometimes we don't see anything at all. We do have to pay attention to notice. In the moments of meditation, however, we are working only on ourselves, so we are an audience of one. It can be hard to stay on track without some outside affirmation that we are on the right path . . . a miracle, perhaps? Sometimes we do manifest miracles, but just because we don't doesn't mean no one's listening.

The Tapestry of Connection

After a while, I came up with my own metaphor to help me understand this connection to all others. I have come to think of my place in the universe to that of a single thread that helps hold a very large tapestry together, except my thread is completely unique in shape, size, and strength. There is only one spot that this thread will fit in order for the tapestry to continue to weave itself. No other thread will do. First, I must find my place. Then I must weave my thread in just such a way that it knits with the other threads around it, making the knots strong and powerful. My particular location in the tapestry cannot be replaced by any other thread, just mine. For obvious reasons, then, no one thread is more important than the next one. They are all equally beautiful, and each is perfectly designed to fit in its own special spot.

I like this metaphor because it emphasizes our uniqueness, which we already know is essential for God's grand creation plan. Remember we bring a "one of a kind" look to whatever it is we are creating. The connection to the tapestry will never be finished until all souls can find their spot and link in. Rest assured, the tapestry will be finished one day, but not until everyone is on board. As this process continues, the tapestry will wait, delay, work around, etc., until those other unique threads show up.

As I was learning all about this grand connection to each other, I started to wonder how I could learn to connect to others better. How can I help out? What should I be doing to move things along? I suddenly felt a responsibility to the collective and struggled to find how I could help.

How to Contribute

I started to really read the news, watch TV, and peruse the internet to see if there was anything I could do to help out. What cause, what organization, what movement should I participate in or donate money to effect change? Nothing seemed to resonate. I just couldn't imagine how I, being so small, could make an impact. I was at a standstill. As I continued to read, I noticed I was getting a very consistent message. It definitely pointed me in the right direction, but it was so simple, I nearly missed it.

> *"This is an* inside *job! The key to making a difference is to heal self and make room for love of self, love for others, and love for God."*
>
> **—Mandy Hale**

It took a while to figure out. It seems I had been operating from a different belief system and needed to make some adjustments. It is so much easier to go out and "do" for others than to "do" for ourselves, isn't it? I sense we lean this way because it does make us feel better. However, are we sure we aren't doing all this good to deliver absolution for our own shortcomings? Personally, I wasn't feeling any "resonance" at all with participating in any way with protest groups or other more active organizations.

Certainly, there is nothing wrong with doing good deeds. A habit of this type of activity might create a transformation of change over a very long period of time . . . or it might produce nothing. We, however, are in a time constraint at this particular time in human evolution. We need more powerful magic to change ourselves, and that magic comes from *inside*. So, if you find yourselves in a quandary about how to contribute, don't fret. There is plenty of improvement to be had in our own personal soul work . . . our Soul Journey.

Religion

The subject of religion is a tricky one in the metaphysical. Religions have proven to be enormously successful in bringing people together for the common good, but something must have gotten lost in translation along the way. The basic truth of all religions is pretty much the same as that in metaphysical cosmology . . . "Love your neighbor as you love yourself." Of course, there is a world of difference in the construct of each religion. Some faiths are centered on Christ, others around Buddha and Yahweh, as examples. As there are many types of people, there are many types of religions that have been established to resonate with particular groups. This is good.

Over mankind's history, however, there have been problems with religion. At what point did religion veer away from the simple rule mentioned above into war-making machines? The Christians have had their Holy Wars, Inquisition, and other not-so-pleasant legacies. Islam has produced warring factions such as ISIS and others, who have twisted loving truths into self-serving beliefs involving jihad, suppression of women, and more. Power, money, and abuse seem to permeate the headlines these days as religions, in general, begin to crumble under the additional weight of unnecessary motivations.

"Where Religion can divide, Spirituality can unite and connect. To find the spiritual core of our religions, we need

to recognize that the whole is more important than the parts
. . . The truth of knowing that we are all one and seek union,
not separation."

—B. Weiss [3]

Religion serves an important purpose because it can connect; it has the ability to bring community together. But without respect for others who worship in a different way and without concern for judgment, it will become increasingly difficult for religious institutions to use their power to unite humans in a meaningful way.

From a personal perspective, I may reconsider my Catholicism the very day the Catholic Church decides that men *and* women are equal and can work together to do God's work. There is not a single valid reason, in my mind, why women can't be priests. What difference does the body make when anyone can deliver love, compassion, and forgiveness in a meaningful way? Tradition or no, *all* of us are capable of divine service in as many unique ways as there are people who would like to do this work. Does it really make sense to toss aside perfectly good workers in the name of tradition? Can we really afford *that* luxury?

I would probably also wait for the church to change its beliefs away from "crime and punishment" to "all is love and forgiveness." If our intent is to match the will of God, then we must understand that we will always be forgiven and we will always have the opportunity to get better. If we need help getting better, we will have it. Truly, it is more God-like to view our spiritual lives this way rather than in personal remorse or fear of punishment over mistakes and unholy deeds. When the churches in the world have elevated themselves to the level of love defined in the Divine universe (and not the earthly one), we will all be on the same page. In the meantime, if you can find this same peace in the quiet, meditative sanctuaries of the church itself, go there to pray. Try to remember that our personal prayers and meditation must always consider our complete connection to each other.

The Age of Aquarius and "The Shift"

"There is a shift happening in humanity, a shift in consciousness, happening now . . . because it has to happen now."

—Eckhart Tolle

The human collective is undergoing a major transformation at this particular time. It has actually been happening for many years now, but 2020 is the first year that the collective has really noticed. There are still many others out there who are unaware. The above quote came to me from an article posted in the *Huffington Post*. This was the first time I had seen or read anything from mainstream media about this shift or shifts even though it has been a heavy focus for those who follow metaphysical news for quite some time.

Awareness of the shift first surfaced in the US on or around the year 2012. This was the end year of a five-thousand-year-old Mayan calendar. Since the last year of the Mayan calendar ended in 2012, everyone thought the world was going to end. It simply marked the end of an age. My personal early awareness that humanity was different was in the 1960s. The hippie movement and their rejection of societal standards reflected the feelings of the "collective" at the time, specifically in response to the Vietnam War and, in general, in response to the gods of power, greed, division, and competition that were (and still are) pervasive at that time. From this place in history came a song from the play *Hair*, performed by The 5th Dimension. The lyrics foretell the dawning of the Age of Aquarius, a wonderful age of heart-love compassion and collective well-being. It appears this prophecy is being fulfilled!

December 21, 2020, marks the first day of the new Age of Aquarius. On this day, the planets of Jupiter, Saturn, and Pluto will form an extremely rare conjunction that will usher in the new age for us. The last Age of Aquarius ended four hundred years ago. It lasted for 2,160 years. The last time all three of these planets were in conjunction was in Capricorn about twenty-five thousand years ago. That was the Age of Capricorn, but the rarity of these planetary alignments is the point. No one living today has ever experienced the age we are soon entering. We are currently leaving the Age of Pisces, which characterizes money, power, control, and invention. We could certainly use a breath of fresh air, and Aquarius, as an Air sign, is ready to deliver.

> *Aquarius represents intellect and ideas. Aquarius is the sign of innovation, technology, and revolution. An Aquarian Age focuses on the collective well-being, logical thought, and innovative growth. This conjunction will spark the beginning of new advancements and technology, medicine, and ideas as well as focus a spotlight on humanitarian issues.*
>
> **—Astrobutterfly.com**

The alignment of planets is not just for our astrological entertainment. In the universe, this is serious business! Every planet, every solar system, every star system will feel the effects of the astrological planetary alignments occurring in December. The energetic effect of such an event is massive. What will it mean for the people of earth? It means we will change, our planet will change, and our lives will change. The greatest effect will be on the inhabitants of this planet and the societal systems in which we have been living. [4]

The Shift

For a long time now, people have been feeling something. We have been suffering here on Earth for quite a while now. The human race is tired. We gave up our free will and are now paying the price. Things are getting more and more out of balance, with the rich getting so much richer and the rest disappearing into poverty. Our freedoms have been compromised. The year 2020 has been front page news for most metaphysics for a couple of decades. This year alone, even prior to the epic conjunction of the three planets in December, we have had and will continue to experience a number of very rare planetary alignments and positions. Below is a list of those that have occurred and are scheduled to occur.

- January 2020: One lunar eclipse and a rare Saturn/Jupiter conjunction. Last time for this was in 1518. Four planets (Pluto, Saturn, Venus, Jupiter, and Pallas, an asteroid) are in Retrograde. (This causes all kinds of delays and setbacks.) Enter Coronavirus.
- April 2020: Mars in Aries in Retrograde. A warlike planet in a warlike sign and both in retrograde, meaning the harshest aspects of the signs are emphasized.
- June 2020: Lunar eclipse, Mercury in Retrograde.
- July 2020: Mercury in Retrograde, Solar eclipse, lunar eclipse.
- November 2020: Election Month! Mars and Mercury in Retrograde. (Another warlike period where Mercury's communication and cooperation aspects are severely challenged.)
- December 2020: The Age of Aquarius. Jupiter, Saturn, and Pluto in Aquarius all in conjunction! A massive solar flare is expected on this day.

No wonder we are tired! Despite the worldwide quarantine, however, the collective today has not been idle. After a few months of "getting used" to our lack of freedom, I sense and notice that people seem to be, well, more content somehow. Yes, it has been a horrible time; people have lost loved ones and their jobs. Our lives have been turned upside down . . . the effect of all those planetary alignments . . . and many of us wish for things to get back to "normal." But in the midst of it all, there has been a change, a heart-opening at the individual level that is growing and swelling in the collective. We are showing concern for others. We have been doing our best to help out. People seem more compassionate and caring about each other and their lives. We are becoming more aware of how we have contributed to the distress of others. BLM is a perfect example of this. Racism is insidious. Many of us behave in racist ways solely because of the culture we were raised in. We never thought we were racist, but the story from the other side is different. We can display racism without even knowing we do it. Those responses are being brought to our attention. They are real! And I see people really trying to change this. It is enlightening.

The Fifth Dimension

The biggest news from the metaphysical world is that this earth is in the midst of an ascension into the fifth dimension from the third. Our entire planet is shifting into a new dimension! Death from ascension is not in the plan. No one has to die since this will be a physical ascension. Everything but the kitchen sink goes. This is also the first time any planet in any solar system will have had this experience. It is to be a major galactic event and a universal headliner when it occurs. We will have audiences, many of them, and most of them will not be from earth. Finally, we will have full disclosure that we have *not* existed in this entire universe alone! Twenty twenty-one has been identified as the year of disclosure, and as of this writing, there have been numerous headlines and photos of alien spacecraft in our skies.

"New Earth" discussions and predictions could fill a volume of encyclopedias. I felt it was important to bring this up now since I know it is happening. I would like to emphasize two things. 1) The fifth dimension is a heart-conscious dimension. Unlike earth, which could be considered a mental/emotional dimension, the fifth dimension is one of no lessons, no karma, no illness, and no suffering. 2) No one is forced to go. All will be given a choice. If you live and love through your heart and all that you do benefits others, then you have heart-consciousness. If you are unwilling to give up the "pleasures" of the earthly world such as things, money, power, control, etc., you will likely choose not to go. It is up to each and every one of us.

There is only one caveat to this great event happening. It is *only* through our human collective that this change happens. A critical mass of humanity has to be on board for this change to occur! It takes a massive amount of energy to make this kind of move. It will be our human collective, filled with heart-conscious love, that will provide this energy. This is why it is so important to realize how critically important our connection to each other really is. We need to put our skills to work. Start working on that heart consciousness. (This is really what a soul journey is all about.) What better time to dust off those books and start thinking about a spiritual path that will make the road a little smoother? It always comes around to what we are feeling in our hearts and what the collective is feeling as it shows its love for humanity. We are well on our way to getting this done! There will be much pushback in the early years. This won't be easy, but we are on target. See you in the fifth! [5] [6]

> *"In the midst of hate, I found there was within me, an invincible love. In the midst of tears, I found there was within me, an invincible smile. In the midst of chaos, I found there was, within me, an invincible calm. I realized, through it all, that in the midst of winter I found there was, within me, an invincible summer. And that makes me happy. For it says that no matter how hard the world pushes you, within me, there is something stronger—something better, pushing right back."*
>
> —Albert Camus

The Journal: Family Circle

We did not leave for Circle until the morning after our families arrived the day or night before. While we were driving down the mountain that morning, our families were being briefed about the objectives and structure of Circle. They had their own workbooks to complete prior to our arrival.

We rode that last trip into town in silence. All of us thinking, "How will it go?" All of us a little nervous. As we were driving down, I was grateful for the fact that I was allowed to participate in this activity at all. I had joined the group about two weeks late, due to my high school graduation activities. Technically, I was to stay in the field for six weeks before being eligible for Circle. But I had spent a month with my tribe, and we all became very close. The next Family Circle would not be for eight more weeks, and by then, I would be at school.

Staff was hesitant about letting me participate early, but logistics ruled, so they decided to let me attend. I agreed to finish my last two weeks back out in the field after Family Circle was over. It was a small price to pay to participate with my group in this most important activity. I figured, after seeing my family, two weeks more would fly by in a blink.

We arrived about noontime, really dirty and really grubby. None of that mattered. When I saw my mom and dad and sister, I felt like my heart would burst. They immediately surrounded me with hugs, love, and kisses. Oh, sweet bliss! I was finally home! No one cared about my appearance. Even Mom didn't say anything about my scruffy "faux" beard. (The men in our family do not look good in facial hair . . . well, according to Mom, anyway.) It really didn't matter. We were all together. We had a family lunch with the group and got a chance to catch up a bit before we were to start at one p.m.

There were a lot of people there! My Quest group consisted of seven students, so we had a good size to begin with. There was no real limit to the number of family members that could attend, but those that showed up were immediate family members. One of our members had five brothers and sisters. They *all* showed up, including the parents and the grandparents. Many families, like mine, were smaller . . . two parents and a sibling or two. Either way, this was a big group.

We entered a large meeting room with chairs for everyone arranged in a large circle. Each person had a view of everyone else. There was water and about a gazillion Kleenex boxes strategically placed. I was a little surprised at this, but it didn't take long to figure out why so many Kleenex boxes were needed! This promised to be a pretty intense meeting.

As we all got settled, we were introduced to our facilitator. Celeste was an older woman, probably in her fifties with gray hair, a dog, and a somewhat "wilderness-like" appearance. She was a psychologist, facilitator, and mystic all rolled up into one powerful human. She was clearly of the earth and almost shamanistic in her ability to intuit and read people. She felt "grandmotherly" and safe. It became clear, however, after the sessions started that she had complete control over the process. There were some pretty ugly moments to come, and Celeste's grace and skill in bringing everyone home was impressive.

Mentioned before, all of us, including our families, had "list work" to do. We prepared our talking points around appreciations, non-appreciations, cleaning the slate, and where we wanted each relationship to go. Each member of my group had spent three days working on their list. In return, our families had to prepare their own lists of appreciations, non-appreciations, and where they wanted our relationship to go. There was no limit to how much time we had or how long our lists had to be. When we were done, we were done.

After Celeste's introduction and instructions, our families took their seats in the Circle. The first person on deck was . . . thankfully, not me! The student would bring a chair and from inside the circle set it right in front of the family member they were addressing. No cross talk was allowed during list work. Each family member had to sit in silence while their child or sibling communicated all the qualities of their relationship, both good and bad, from their perspective.

When finished with one family member, the student would move his chair in front of the next member and go through the same process again. No one was interrupted before their time. After the student completed his part, each family member then took a seat in the chair inside the circle and faced the student with their list of appreciations and non-appreciations. In some cases, it took forty-five minutes or more for a family to finish this phase of Circle. It was going to be a long day.

The magic of Circle was the connection we all had to this specific event. None of the families knew anyone else, but this public witnessing of cleansing was powerful to all who attended. We were all there for the same reasons. We had that in common.

It was hard to hear other families articulate what our own family went through. Many times a student would bring something up that either I or a family member forgot to mention during our time, and this brought fresh pain back home.

We certainly weren't "done" after our individual Circle time. Compassion over the pain of others was instantaneous. While the stories were different, we all went through various iterations of something the same. We understood each other's pain. After four weeks in the field, I certainly knew the pain of my tribe members. I knew my parents would relate to the pain other parents had regarding the addictions of their child. We all knew how it felt, no matter the source. The energy in the room radiated love despite the pain.

Probably the most difficult part of Circle was "cleaning the slate." As a liar, there was a *lot* my family didn't know. There were a lot of risky situations I got myself into that I had decided, in the past, never to mention. I had to bring it up. I had to go for broke. I wanted a new life. I was scared. Since most of my lying had to do with my self-image and fitting in, I knew that cleaning the slate might trash my fragile house of cards. But I was willing to take the risk. This had to work!

My family alone went through one whole box of Kleenex, all by themselves, and this was before I was even on deck.

When it was my turn, I was ready. I sat through at least four other family discussions. Most went pretty well, so I was encouraged. Celeste had done an amazing job of keeping everyone on point, particularly since the situation was so emotional. It was late by the time I started, but no one was really tired. Wrung out, maybe, but not really tired. I started my circle at about ten p.m.

I was so proud of my family. I did most of my cleaning the slate facing Mom. She was the one who shouldered the burden of my choices for eighteen years, and she deserved to hear honesty from me for the first time in my life. She was so open, so stoic during my presentation. She didn't seem upset about anything I mentioned . . . even my sexual experiences at a relatively young age. She was bathing herself in my truth for the first time and didn't seem to mind what that truth was. I know her. She was just so glad to see this side of me. I think it was all she ever wanted.

When it was my family's turn to clean the slate, I was surprised. Mom, who mightily resisted going to Al-Anon during my rehab days, revealed some personal discoveries on codependent behavior, which she really didn't understand during that time . . . probably because she didn't spend enough time with Al-Anon.

Either way, somehow in putting together her list, she experienced a sublime moment of insight and awareness and realized how she had contributed to the situation. I knew she was devastated over this knowledge. She apologized for not letting me take karate lessons with Edward when I was six because it was "too violent" and Edward and I played too many violent games. She was finally seeing the impact of trying to protect someone else from something she personally experienced. She told me she was so sorry for squashing the "real" me, despite her good intentions.

Of course, I know I am responsible for my own behavior. But, I tell you, her words were like honey to me. I really like my mom a lot, and to see this honest self-awareness brought hope and clarity and love back into my life.

My sessions with Dad and my sister also went well. My dad is not much of a communicator, but he did a good job on his part. He apologized for "stepping away" during the gnarly early days of my addictions and rehab. Dad is such a good man. It's easy to take him for what he is. He is the quiet strength that has bonded this family together. He doesn't say much, but he never left us, and he never got in the way of what had to be done. I want to have a really close relationship with him, just like with Mom.

My sister was very young at the time, having just finished sixth grade. I had no idea how much she looked up to me. I'm sorry I ignored her, despite her bratty ways. I look forward to really getting to know her. She is pretty sweet.

After my turn was over, I was on cloud nine! I didn't imagine it could go this well. I'm not sure how one can reinspire inspiration, but that's what happened. My heart was so full and my resolve to stay the course so strong, I felt euphoric. I took some time to bask in the glow.

By the time we finished Circle that first day, it was three a.m. I got to stay at the hotel across the street with my family, but we had to be back at Circle by eight a.m. the next morning. We still had a few more families to go through. Sleeping in a real bed was the icing on the cake.

The next morning we got up really early and walked over to the breakfast café for food. It was a hole-in-the-wall dive, but I never tasted anything so good! Living on powdered eggs for a month caused me to forget what the real deal tasted like. Mom was dumbstruck. She basically hadn't seen me eat for about two years. I wouldn't or couldn't . . . it depended on the situation. She was used to it, but when she saw me at breakfast, she was overjoyed. The coffee was mighty good, too!

We arrived at the meeting room a little before eight a.m. and settled in our seats. Celeste welcomed the group, made some inspiring comments about the work that was done the day before, and reinstructed the group on the process, just in case anyone forgot. The Kleenex boxes had been refreshed.

There were three more families that still had to go. I was so glad we were done with our session. I was full, relaxed, and happy. I found myself much more attentive to the dynamics of the other family sessions. One of those on deck for their turn this day was my buddy with the extra-large family.

This session took up the better part of the morning. Each brother, sister, mom, dad, and both grandparents had to be addressed. The love that filled up that corner of the room felt like a living, breathing thing. I was a little jealous because of this. I had always wanted a bigger family, but Mom was the oldest of six kids and didn't think a really big family added much benefit . . . particularly when there wasn't much time to give the kind of attention she felt everyone deserved. But when a family is filled with so much love, it can't be all bad.

As the youngest of the five siblings, my buddy got a lot of attention. It was attention I know he didn't necessarily want, but then none of us really wanted this kind of attention, either, particularly when we were doing "our thing." He did a good job, but there were issues with his dad. Some of this came up out in the field, but until you see the players, you can't really understand what is really going on.

When he got to his dad to share his appreciations and non-appreciations, he closed up. He just couldn't go on.

Celeste, in her wisdom, asked him to sit in his dad's lap. The room was atwitter. Some uncomfortable shuffling and readjusting in seats was going on. My friend was incredulous, thinking this might be a joke. When Celeste again asked him to take a seat in his dad's lap, he was hesitant, but he finally relented.

She used a different choice of words when she asked him to address his dad. It didn't take but about five minutes before the entire room was in tears. It was probably one of the most powerful interactions of the entire two days. At the end, it was clear to all of us and my friend that he would be forever enveloped in love and support. All he had to do was make the commitment.

We took a little break after his time was over to collect and refresh ourselves. Next up . . . another heartbreaking truth session. We had one young woman in our group. She was sweet, artistic, intuitive, and smart, but her story was terrifying. As she cleared the slate with her mom, she revealed that her addiction to hard drugs led her to get them any way she could.

One night, she found herself in a really bad part of town, in a rundown apartment trying to score from a dealer she didn't know. The end result was a knife at her throat and the threat of rape. Her mother lost it. She had no idea how bad the situation was. The shock was so strong; she let loose an anguished, heartbreaking wail and fell from her chair to the floor. It took her at least thirty minutes to recover. Celeste handled that part privately in a different room. When she came back, she was much better.

We all knew this was coming. We had worked with our friend very hard in Circles and AA meetings. This was a very painful thing not only for my friend to remember, but to reveal to her mother. She nearly died that night, and she had told no one until our Circles out in the field. I can't imagine living with that kind of terror for so long. She was able to return and finish her appreciations and non-appreciations. Her mom, while shaken, wore an aura of acceptance and love. They would get past this!

It was about three p.m. when we finished Family. The atmosphere was calm, serene, and peaceful. All of us were mentally and emotionally exhausted, but we were filled with hope for wonderful new beginnings. Now that Circle was done, there was a bit more work to do . . . Contracts and Letters.

Reflection

From my view here on the other side, this was indeed a very effective process. In order to get past ourselves and on to expressing our true potential to the world, we have to look in a mirror and face our painful truths. Drugs weren't the first addiction. The first addictions for me were insecurity and a belief that I was different from everyone else and didn't fit in. To compensate, I misbehaved and lied. Surprisingly, this created the attention I craved.

Being the center of attention was an emotional high for me. It didn't matter that the attention wasn't an elevated one. Creating a disturbance along with inappropriate behavior felt good for a little while, until it went away. Then I could start the whole process again. I was recycling old, negative energy over and over. After ten or more years of this, I got pretty good at my deception until I finally threw drugs into the mix. The price was high.

Most addictions, whether mental, physical, or otherwise, are the result of our own personal belief system. The beliefs we hold create behaviors and a personality and physicality that complement the belief. In order to change ourselves, we must first replace the original hard-wired belief with a new one that includes a different vision of who we are. The many weeks I spent in the field gave me the opportunity to decide who I wanted to be and how I wanted to be.

In my heart, I wanted to change what I believed about myself more than anything. I infused that desire for a new me with a self-loving and compassionate emotion. I imagined myself as a stellar college student, with non-using friends who got high on school, sports, computers, and being with friends. I imagined myself *that* person. How would I walk? How would I talk? What would I do? And then . . . the magic ingredient . . . I **felt** the new emotions that would accompany being that new person . . . joy, love, gratitude, appreciation, dignity, power, etc.

In the thirty days I was in the field, I began to believe I was this new person. This is the last step in the process. Change those original limiting beliefs and create greater, more expansive ones. *Feel* how it feels!

The appreciations, non-appreciations and cleaning the slate were the tools we used that day to open up to our families and show them how we had changed. I had spent four weeks in the field working on this, working to create myself as a different person. I understood how this happened, accepted that it did, and resolved to do the work to make the changes. Even if some families didn't see it right off, I knew who we really were, and it wasn't what our families had witnessed in the past. We had to stay the course.

> *"The moment you change your perception is the moment you rewrite the chemistry of your body."*
>
> **—DailyOm.com**

The Journal: Last Steps

We were pretty emotionally wrung out after Family. It was truly a cleansing. For me, it was freeing. I never realized how truly stressful it was to maintain my old lifestyle with the lies and sneaking around. I often forgot which lies I told particularly when the situation was compounded by my drug use. It was hard to keep it all together.

On the other hand, seeing my tribe with their families opened up a Pandora's box of various types and levels of pain that our addictions create for those who care for us the most. While I thought I was affecting my family in only one way, it was clear that I had hurt them on so many different levels. It was a sobering thought . . . no pun intended.

I decided that guilt was a useless emotion to feel in these circumstances. Instead, I decided to embrace my new future with love and fully commit to the process. I knew I could do it, but I was a little scared. The greatest gift I could give myself and my family was my joy in recovery.

Nevertheless, the group was pretty quiet after Family ended. All of us were emotionally resting. It was just as well because our work was not finished for the day. After Family, each of our families was assigned a counselor to work out a schedule of activities designed to keep the essence of the Circle continuing after we left and for when we got home.

For me, I had to develop a ninety-day aftercare plan that I would follow when I got to Chico. The biggest challenge would be to fill my schedule. It's no joke that idle time creates a problem mind. If you don't have an outlet for your boredom, it's too easy to go back to what you know . . . not an option for me. I had to create the outline of a life that would assure I was too busy to relapse. Either that or learn how to fill dead time with some creative activity or thinking. I decided that, at this stage, it was far easier just to make a schedule to deal with dead time.

In addition to my course work, I planned to join a number of athletic clubs. I got a bike as a graduation present before I left for Utah, so biking was definitely on my list. I also decided to look at other clubs available to me when I got to school. I really wanted to do something with my computer science skills as well, but I wouldn't be able to take any of the higher-level programming classes until I had finished my prerequisites. I determined that I would start meeting and talking to my professors in the computer science department just to establish myself. Perhaps there would be something I could work on that would put me in the thick of things as I was getting the preliminaries out of the way. I also decided to resume my Team Xbox writing.

As if this weren't enough, I committed to AA every day. I also resolved to get a sponsor. Not on the official list, but on my list, was learning to pray. I was still seeking that special connection to God and knew I needed him in my life. I just wasn't sure how this would look.

Just to make sure we hadn't forgotten all we learned and the struggles we went through, I had to create a list of triggers, people and places I needed to avoid. I left my meeting with the belief and feeling that I had a good plan and that it was structured enough for me to execute. I covered all my bases. The most important thing I would leave this place with was the conviction that I had already changed and that I already was becoming very familiar with the new me . . . a pretty cool kid on his own with no enhancements.

My family, as well, had to create and commit to their own personal contracts. Mom resolved to attend Al-Anon, and it was decided that we would have our own family circle each Sunday, via phone, after I left for school. We decided that we would set a time for this. Everyone had to be available, and we would pattern our conversation on the honesty and openness we experienced in Family. We were given great communication tools during this experience, and we all resolved to emulate them.

The last thing for me to do then was to write my goodbye letters. This was hard, very hard. I wrote two letters: one to drugs, the crutches that held me back, and one was to the friends I used with in order to fit in. I knew that putting my words to paper would seal the deal. I was sad writing them, especially the ones to my friends, but what I really noticed was the sense of relief I felt when I wrote them. This was really the end.

Family was over. The culmination of four weeks of hard labor, mental work, emotional work, and spiritual work all came together to make this event powerful. And powerful it was! I saw my family completely differently. Of course, extreme homesickness made being away from them initially more painful, but after that passed, all I had left were images of each of them and how truly loving they really were. I wanted to go home! However, I had a commitment for two more weeks. I was a little sad that I wouldn't be going home with them, but oddly, I was anxious to get back out in the field. Two weeks is nothing compared to how I felt when I left home for this adventure. Then six weeks seemed like an eternity . . . especially since I didn't get much warning and had to scrap all my summer plans. But had I known how it would turn out and how different I would feel, the time would have never bothered me.

That night I got another night in the hotel room in a real bed *and* a massive steak dinner! Parting is such sweet sorrow, but a steak makes it all good! Of course I also had the wonderful experience of being clean (as in taking a bath) for the first time in a month. Cheap hotel showers rule the day. So many appreciations!

The next morning we got up around eight a.m., had breakfast, and headed over to headquarters. I had a little time to say goodbye to my tribe since they would be going home with their families. We exchanged addresses and phone numbers so we could stay in touch. I had to jet out to the mountain as the Jeep was waiting. I kissed my mom and dad and sister adieu for only fourteen more days and headed off into the sunset. They had a long four-hour drive to the airport and on to home.

When I got back to camp, I met my new group with a level of confidence and openness that I didn't know I had mastered. I felt so different. The group was newly formed so there was a lot of that initial pushback or the full-out shutting down that we all exhibited in my group. It's funny, when you're in it, you feel so justified in your anger and resentment. When you step outside and experience a Family Circle and then return, the picture is jarring.

I knew things these people didn't know. I didn't realize how much I did know. I felt nothing but compassion for them and the situation, but I knew because of my experience that I might be able to bring a little hope and an expectation that this experience will truly change them . . . if they open up and let it.

So when I shared in Circle and AA, I truly shared! I abandoned the slick talk and the "prototype" persona. I came as me, warts and all, and as always when I did this, I opened even more and learned even more. I listened hard to their stories and was able to comment and provide feedback in meaningful ways. I felt more like a mentor than a participant, and I liked it.

It feels different when you live to serve and to help others. This was a new feeling for me, and it made me feel worthy and whole. I held off leading any hikes unless personally asked. I had mastered these skills in the time I was in the field, and I knew that it was important for each person in the group to do the same. I wouldn't take that away from any of them.

The counselors welcomed my participation and encouraged more of it. I was helping the members of this group in my own small way, but it was a positive experience. It was during this time that I decided that I would return to the program the following summer as a counselor in training. I wanted to do this again, but from the other side.

My Journey to Understand

I was not privy to any information on the spirituality of connection when I attended the formal family circle that capped Patrick's Wilderness Quest experience. I honestly didn't know what to expect. I just wanted to see him, and I wanted him home. Despite this, all of us were looking forward to being there.

My personal experience with Family was nothing short of an epiphany. The lack of sleep and intense personal emotional work served to place me in an altered state of reception . . . and this just from my own personal work! Bearing witness to the pain and traumas of the other families involved, however, opened up my heart in ways I had never experienced. I feel I emerged transformed. I believe it was one of the most important experiences of my life. I came home renewed and overjoyed. I had my son back.

Just how effective the entire Wilderness Quest experience was for my son is chronicled in the detail of his life post-Wilderness Quest. Patrick took his new self to college in a cloud of new expectations and adventure. He made new friends, different friends. He immersed himself in his studies and his passion for computers. I never saw him happier.

While the events of Patrick's life after Wilderness Quest can be relegated to the "normal" category, it is easy to identify the nuances of change in how he went about his days. I viewed everything at this time as a miracle. Patrick's journal that follows continues with life, after his WQ soul journey. I add this section to demonstrate that any soul journey, which might or might not include wonderful prayer and meditation practices, always shows growth from new knowledge and the understanding that comes with it. The difficult part is the daily application of these new truths and ideas to our life. This is where the rubber meets the road. If we can't apply all the beautiful information we are getting to *change* how we view and approach each day, then we have learned nothing at all. Transformation is hard and requires persistence! How Patrick approached his new life at Chico was a world of a different color than how he approached his life during his high school years.

The Journal

Goodbye, Moab!

Fastest two weeks ever! I took my time while I had nature at my back and the blessed silence that came with it to rehearse the new me. While I occasionally had some niggling doubts about my ability to stay sober, I quickly brushed that insecurity away and imagined someone with absolute confidence of complete success. I could do this! I knew it.

I was so excited about going home that I thought I would float away with the fullness I felt. Joy, gratitude, love . . . so many wonderful emotions flowing through my body. I had transformed myself physically, mentally, emotionally, and spiritually in six weeks' time. I was definitely not the same person as when I left. I really liked the new me. I was physically the fittest I had ever been. I enjoyed the strength and stamina I was experiencing. Truly, I had no idea how weak my physical level was until I healed myself. It was a tad scary. I never want to feel that way again!

I was a little insecure, though, about how I would make new friends. I had only known one way to do it. As much as the program helped me and despite the fact I made friends here, it was a controlled environment. We were all going our separate ways, and it was unknown if we would ever have contact with each other again. Intellectually, I understood that college would also be a new environment and somewhat controlled, so I shouldn't have worried too much . . . but a little worry crosses every neophyte's mind from time to time. I decided the decision I made was a good one and then also decided to stop worrying about it and let it go. I needed to trust myself.

In the meantime, I would enjoy being with my family again. I woke up early the last morning I would be in Utah. I showered, shaved, ate breakfast, and packed my bags. I spent some time talking to the counselors and others who were there for my send off.

I told Karen and Larry that I wanted to come back the following summer as a counselor in training. They were more than welcoming. And then I walked across the street and waited for my bus. I would have four hours to rest, reflect, and just think thoughts until I got to the airport. As I gazed out the bus windows, I remember that beautiful moon I saw on the bus trip out here. This truly is a magical place.

Home at Last

I arrived at SFO in the late afternoon. The whole gang was there to pick me up . . . Mom, Dad, my sister, and Bailey, our dog. The homecoming in front of the very busy, very stressful baggage claim pick-up was quite the display. Everyone jumped out of the car to hug me, greet me, kiss me, and get my bags. We were all so excited. The curbside cop was trying to be respectful, but we had to move on. Bailey, who was still in the car, was so excited there was not one part of his body that wasn't shaking, wagging, hopping, moving, or licking. When we got settled, he sat in my lap with his nose to my nose. He just stared. It was good to be home!

Pulling into the driveway, seeing my home for the first time in six weeks seemed surreal. It's almost as if it were a dream. Out in Utah, all this seemed so far away. It had felt like a very distant memory. But things were exactly as I left them. Only the feeling I brought home with me this day was different than any other time I left the house and later returned. I had enormous gratitude for the gift I had been given. Everything looked brighter and warmer and felt so, so safe. I had truly come home, heart and all.

The next few weeks were spent preparing for Chico. My mom had to pre-enroll me while I was away so I could get into some of the more popular but required general ed classes. I reviewed these classes, decided to make a few changes, and turned my attention to packing. I didn't contact my old party buddies at all when I got home. They didn't really know when I left or exactly where I had gone. I didn't have the courage to tell them the truth before I left. I am also sorry to say I didn't really even know where some of these guys were going to school.

I knew a couple of them also got accepted to Chico. I wasn't sure if they would be there, but I was reasonably assured that they would probably be staying in the college dorms on campus if this was their school. I don't know why I was so sure of this, but I was. I was not going to stay in the campus dorm. Instead, Mom signed me up for University Village, which was a private dormitory off-campus. It had slightly larger rooms with a mini kitchen and private bath. I had signed up for a two-man room.

Chico!

The weekend we were to report to campus was also family orientation weekend. Mom, Dad, my sister, and my uncle Kurt all came with and planned to spend the weekend attending orientation events and getting me moved in. Mom invited her brother, Kurt, to join us on this trip because he was also in recovery. Kurt had been in AA a long time and was successfully sober. He was going to help me find a decent AA meeting, and perhaps, if there was time, we could connect with a mentor. In our free time, we explored the beautiful little town of Chico and all it had to offer.

I was excited to be here. The town was awesome, and we were surrounded by nothing but mountains, hills, and other wide-open spaces. There were hiking trails, the Sacramento River, wading pools, waterfalls, and all kinds of nature stuff. I reasoned that if I ever needed to get another big dose of the outdoors, this place had it all.

When the time came that weekend to move into the dorm, I was beyond excited. We made our way to the village and my room. There was a sign on the door that had my name and my roommate's name on it. When we walked into the room, Chris had already moved in. He wasn't there at that exact moment, but I cursed myself for not getting there first. We had a bunk bed, and he took the lower one. The upper bunk was actually the one I preferred, so it wasn't a big deal. I know, I know, it's just that I was slightly disgruntled I didn't get there first.

It didn't take too long to get moved in. I found a prime spot for my computer and Xbox and set up a play station in front of the sofa that apparently belonged to Chris. I knew what one of my college activities was going to be, and that was Xbox games!

Now maybe this whole video game playing thing towards which I invested a good portion of my life could have been considered a "gateway" drug to the real deal, but this was something I was *not* going to give up. Computers and video games were my passion, and I fully expected to spend the rest of my life playing, developing, or creating more to feed the passion. I had no idea how Chris would feel about this since I hadn't even met him yet.

Soon, Chris and his mom arrived. He seemed like a really nice kid. He was local, living an easy drive from home to school. My first impression of Chris was that he was quite shy. He seemed nervous. He was very quiet, and he stayed near his mom. Well, I was nervous, too, but was pretty good at hiding that, so I tried to make Chris a little more comfortable with my effervescent personality.

I actually liked Chris a whole lot. He only had one flaw. He was an Apple guy. The worst! Macs are fine for the novice. They can do just about anything . . . at a basic level. However, if you tinker with software and hardware enough, as I did, you need to have a regular PC to do anything fancy. I had partially rebuilt the computer I used for gaming, and the display, graphics, and response time were clearly at another level. In addition, owning a PC also meant you could load way more sophisticated software. Apple only does Apple stuff. Chris loved his computer, though, and resisted any kind of effort to see reason. It didn't matter. I would have the whole year to convert him.

As much as I love my family, I couldn't wait for them to leave so I could get to the business of living my life. I think a lot of the freshmen walking around campus that weekend had the same thoughts. The excitement of moving onto a college campus that everyone experienced the first day was replaced by some somber, surly attitudes by day three, the last day. I discovered even myself making a little distance between me and my family as we were walking around town.

Classes wouldn't start for another week, so I had lots of time to explore. Chris got more comfortable and invited some of his high school friends over to the room. Blake was Chris' best friend at the time, and he lived in the dorm room above ours and not too far away. Blake came over with a couple of buddies, and we spent a fine time getting acquainted.

My days that week were spent getting the lay of the land. I needed to find where my classes were, where the good restaurants and eating places were, and what was happening on campus. Some of this I did on my own, the rest with Chris and a few hanger-ons that just wanted to walk the town.

The first week of school was also a huge party week. I had played with the idea of going to the river for a day of mixing it up with several hundred or even a thousand fellow students. I knew there would be a lot of drinking so thought better of this plan . . . for this year, anyway. It didn't matter much because there were plenty of people that stayed behind and took to the village swimming pool. It was while I was there that I got some news that just put me in a tizzy.

I found out that a few of my old high school drinking buddies were actually living at University Village! This was not good. I was angry. I wasn't going to let them get me back to where I was in high school. This just ticked me off!

Later on that evening, I called my mom and told her what I learned. She got the full vent of my rage. Her response was surprising but not altogether unexpected, I suppose. She asked me to calm down and then quietly told me that this is a free country. People can live where they want. Remember, she told me, your friends do not know what you did this summer and why. This was your challenge, which you successfully completed. Yes, you achieved what you wanted to achieve, but it takes effort to stay on top. You don't get to coast.

Well, when you put it like that, I guess I overreacted a bit. I was just annoyed, that's all. I wanted my bliss all to myself. And I realized another thing . . . I was responsible for my drinking, not my friends. There really was no way they could get me to do drugs and drink again if I didn't want it.

Bike!

One of the new activities I took up right away was riding my new bike. I didn't get much bike riding in at home because the roads were too remote and hilly and too far away from anything fun. I did enjoy riding my bike around campus especially since I lived half a mile away. Biking was freeing! At least for two weeks it was freeing. I came home one day and discovered the bike was gone! Thinking it was stored safely behind the six-foot wall of our small balcony, someone apparently reached over and just took it. Really?

Of course the incident involved a lot of drama. Chris, me, and others took to searching the entire complex to find my bike. Everyone was a suspect. Chris started to freak out because he thought we might have a stalker. At the end of the day, I gave up. I expected to be teased.

Chris eventually got over his jitters, and the incident was forgotten, until he returned from a weekend home visit with a brand new, expensive ten-speed! I couldn't believe it. It was like the stolen bike incident never happened. A plan was forming in my head.

I decided to let Chris bond with his bike for a week or so. It was difficult since his bragging about the bike was getting annoying. And then, one dark and stormy night . . . well, maybe the weather was better . . . I placed said bike in the shower. I did not do this alone. I had conspirators. Chris came home for the day, and we were waiting. He didn't notice his bike was missing. Getting impatient, my posse and I started to talk about his bike. *Then* he noticed it was gone! He flipped out. He was distraught. He was starting to sweat. I suggested he calm down, take a shower, relax. He was so busy twirling and pacing with deep worry to take my advice. He left to look around the complex. When he got back, he was really sweaty! I again suggested he take a shower. Finally, he complied.

It was worth the wait! The screams of shock and joy were quickly replaced by indignation. We laughed until we couldn't anymore. This was a very good day.

Campus Life

It didn't take but a couple of weeks for news of my Team Xbox play station to get around. Chris and others did their best to beat me, but this was my life and nothing or no one could take me down as top dog. Our room was the place to go for recreational playing and organized game playing. The Xbox kept me out of a lot of trouble.

College classes, for the most part, felt so adult to me. No one cared if you showed up or not. I was too old to be disruptive in class and, somehow, had lost the inclination to be so. Gosh, I guess I was maturing. This couldn't have happened at a better time, since I emerged from the mountains of Utah with a completely clean slate. I arrived as a blank pallet in Chico to create a new me. High school antics were definitely out of here!

In the meantime, I was making inroads with the professors in the engineering department "meet and greets" and office visits. There were a number of computer and engineering clubs and groups my professors referred to me. If I couldn't get to the higher-level programming classes because of the math requirements this year, I would get my fix some other way, and this seemed like a good start.

My first semester was packed with classes. There really was no time for much else. Of course, Team Xbox reviews were also on my plate. I found I didn't have too much difficulty organizing myself. This was kind of a surprise to me since Mom took over *all* my organizing when I was growing up.

I decided when classes were done for the day; I would come home, take a nap, do my homework, and then write my reviews. This was followed by dinner out with the buds and then a *Halo* game or two back at the room. I was amazed I could fit all this in one day. I had a list of tutors to help in other classes, mainly calculus. I found if I really paid attention I could stay on top of the work, but a tutor would come in handy if I got behind. I had my bases covered.

One of my classes was speech. I do like giving speeches! Our first assignment was to make a persuasive speech. I was so inspired by my argument with Chris on the benefits of a PC over a Mac that I made it my topic. I pretended like I didn't know Chris was in the room when I was practicing it. The act itself was entirely satisfying. I got an A-.

The programming class was very basic and started at the beginning. I knew the material from past experience, but it was a good review. When we finally got into actual programming assignments, it was pretty easy at this level. When I did come across a problem that stumped me, all I needed to do was take a little nap with the problem on my mind and I would wake up with the answer! This used to really get Mom going. She wanted in the worst way to be able to take a little nap to solve her problems and wake up with the answer. My dad has this ability. I'm lucky I inherited it. It does come in handy!

Girlfriend!

I met Joanne just after we had all moved in and our families had left. Classes hadn't started yet. I was puttering in my room when I heard some people at the door. Chris and I usually left it open since we had visitors dropping by all day long.

On this particular day, Chrissy, who lived upstairs, came by with a friend. Chrissy was looking for Blake, Chris's best high school friend. It was obvious she had a crush on him. Blake wasn't there, but I invited them in anyway. I immediately noticed her friend, who was a gorgeous Filipina American. She and I made eye contact, and well . . . I don't know . . . there was just something. She introduced herself as Joanne.

Now I had met a couple of girls earlier, and they were nice. We had some fun, but Joanne was just different. For one, she was Filipino. This in itself was unusual as Chico was a pretty white-washed college at the time. I thought about this later, but at the time I didn't notice anything unusual, except she was Filipino and that just felt normal to me . . . probably because of my experience with Edward and his family. Joanne also seemed very shy.

She scanned the room, and I saw her pause when she got to my computer. She immediately walked over to get a better look. "Nice computer," she said. "I see you have Alienware loaded up. What's it for?"

Whoa! Alrighty then! Who is this sweet, young thing that can recognize a rebuilt computer loaded with Alienware?! I told her about my Team Xbox avocation and why I built the computer the way I did. She nodded knowingly and then proceeded to tell me how she spent the summer rebuilding her motherboard. Am I in heaven or what?!! I need to get to know this girl!

We had a week before classes started, and the University Village was still holding a lot of orientation meetings regarding life there. I attended as many meetings as I could because I often saw Joanne there. It was through these "accidental" meetings that I was able to attract her interest. By this time, she had earned the nickname Panda because she was in the habit of roaming the complex in her Panda PJs. The nomer suited her perfectly. We would chat over nothing, but she was just so cute. Afterward, Joanne and me and a group of others would wander into the village for a snack or a walk.

My relationship with Joanne seemed to be moving at warp speed. It was a little while later that we were intimate, but before that, we were joined at the hip. We went into town together, ate together, and took walks. For all her shyness, Joanne was quite the talker. I was, too, so this was a very cool relationship. For some reason, I felt I could be as open and honest as possible with her. I had never had a relationship with a girl on this basis. In high school, sex was pretty much the driving factor, and I often found myself dumped shortly thereafter. Of course, these incidents were precipitated by much drinking and using, so I'm not sure why I would expect anything different. Either way, it left me with a negative impression of girls. I was a bit insecure in this area.

Joanne put me at ease. She was so nonjudgmental. It was at least a month before I laid all my history on the table. Though I noticed that Joanne was not a drinker, I didn't bring up my sobriety until this time. I told her I considered myself an alcoholic. I told her about rehab in high school, and I told her about Wilderness Quest. It was the Wilderness Quest experience that really impressed her. She was fascinated by my process of self-discovery in nature, group therapy, the people in my tribe, the workbooks, and the journal. I was proud of my accomplishments, and she really seemed to appreciate all of it.

I was so worried she would run away. As the weeks flew by, we shared everything. She never flinched. She never bolted. She was my best friend, and she was a girl! Now, that is progress! By the end of the month, I gave her the turquoise ring that Dad had given me a few years before. Dad told me all the men in the Kolsky family had turquoise rings, and I told Panda I wanted her to have mine. She was to consider it a "pre-engagement" ring. There was no doubt in my mind that this was the girl I was going to marry.

Meeting the Parents

I didn't tell my family about Joanne except that I met her at school and wanted to bring her home for a visit. I didn't even tell them that she was Filipina American. I didn't do this "on purpose" because the difference wasn't that obvious to me. The first nine years of my life was spent as another member of Edward's household. As we well know, I enjoyed this part of my life the best. Joanne symbolized all of these happy memories and more.

I was nervous but should have realized that my family would love Joanne. Perhaps she was a little too quiet, but I didn't realize how nervous she was until after we left. Mom loved her and thought she was gorgeous.

Anthony, Blake's roommate, me, and Joanne all showed up one beautiful weekend in October. Anthony had the wheels so he would drive. My mom was planning to take a large group of Lauren's friends to the Renaissance Faire to celebrate her birthday. Her birthday is really in December, but that is not a good time to do a field trip, so it was to happen in October. We had a grand time. Mom and Joanne made flower garlands for the girls, and we spent the afternoon pretending we were knights and maidens. I was pleased with everything that day, especially with how much my family liked Joanne.

Thanksgiving

Thanksgiving in the year 2002 was going to be a little different than normal. Both my mom and dad have relatively large extended families . . . Dad was number three of four siblings, and Mom was number one of six. Since most of the family members lived within commuting distance, there was always a place to go, with family members sharing hosting duties.

Frank, my dad's older brother, lives in St. George, Utah. This year, he and his wife, Michele, extended an invitation to all of Dad's family, including some cousins and others from Kansas, to celebrate Thanksgiving at their place. I was really looking forward to it. For one, it was the first ever and only road trip my family would take together.

The plan was to drive up to Chico from the Bay Area, pick me up, then drive back down Interstate 5 to Las Vegas, where we would spend the night. The next morning we would have maybe a ninety-minute drive to St. George. The second reason I was excited is because I would get another opportunity to visit Utah, the land of dreams for me.

Heavenly Hindsight

The universe indeed moves in interesting ways. Frank and Michele, who did not have children of their own, had not considered hosting Thanksgiving at their place in the past. This year they decided to do it. It would be the very last time I would see them in this life. The event was a momentous one as it was our time to say hello again . . . and goodbye. When coincidental events like this line up thusly, rest assured they are likely part of a plan and are meant to occur. We don't always know the reasons in life, but the answers are very clear in the life beyond life.

The Journal

Vegas Layover and St. George

We made it down to Vegas in about eleven hours. It was a fun ride and a beautiful day. I had a chance to really talk to my family about school and Joanne and my hopes and dreams. It was so good to be with them. We ate a good meal, toodled around the casino, and had a good night's sleep. We were to leave the next morning for St. George.

It wasn't long before we were out of Vegas and back into the desert. I was feeling at home again. I do love this part of the country. As the miles flew by, the desert morphed from sand, Joshua trees, and tumbleweeds into a different kind of desert. Finally, the terrain changed from flat to hills to changing desert shrubs to the ultimate crowning glory ... the red mountains of Utah! Such a sight to behold. Truly gorgeous.

We found my uncle's adobe-like home in a widely spaced neighborhood desert community with a backdrop of big red mountains stretching as far as the eye could see. The weather was also just as beautiful. I was really looking forward to this visit. When we got to the house, there were a lot of people. Most of them I didn't know, but all were relatives. They were from Dad's family, so Grandma and Grandpa were there as well as my cousin, Carol Ann, and her family *and* her boyfriend, whom none of us had met before.

After the meet and greets, we got our house assignment. We were going to stay with Michele's sister, who lived in the same neighborhood close by. We left to get settled in our new digs. It was a beautiful home, as was my uncle's, and very comfortable. During the three days we stayed there, we were free to roam and move from one house to another. One day Mom and Lauren took a horse ride into the mountains, and I hit the red hills for a hike with Dad. It felt good to hike again, and I reminded myself I still hadn't found time to explore the wilderness of Chico. That would go on my bucket list when I got back.

All in all, the entire experience was very wholesome. We played cards, sang karaoke, took hikes, ate amazing food, and got to know each other. This whole feeling of family was lovingly warm. This was something I had not allowed myself to enjoy when I was deep in the mire of drinking and drugs. I really didn't understand what this type of connection really meant. For me, it was safety, belonging, fitting in, and love. Wow. I missed out on a lot, but I planned to make up for it.

On Our Way

Back on the road again and I was assigned driving duties. I suspected Mom was busy paying attention to my driving rather than her memories, so I stayed chill behind the wheel. We got to Bakersfield and decided to call it a day. We would finish the drive to Chico in the morning.

Refreshed and alert the next morning, we took an easy drive and reached Chico sometime that afternoon. I would be seeing everyone again over Christmas break less than a month away. It had been a good trip. I carried a feeling of "fullness" for the next couple of days. It was, indeed, a very good trip.

Home for the Holidays

I was looking forward to coming home! My first semester at Chico had been a good one. I managed to maintain my sobriety . . . for the most part. I did have an occasional beer or two, but the thrill was pretty much gone. I realized I had made a lot of new friends at school and discovered that in no way were any of the friendships I made contingent on participating with altering substances. This was a huge breakthrough!

The only thing I didn't do was find an AA group and attend meetings. In the beginning, this made me nervous because I believed that if I didn't attend these meetings I was at serious risk of relapse. The problem I had was finding a close, convenient meeting. Nothing seemed to work with my schedule. As time played out, I stopped thinking about it and just went about the business of living my new life. I considered AA my backup plan if I slipped. At least it was always there, and that seemed enough to sustain me.

The last three to four weeks of school before the winter break were devoted pretty much exclusively to finals! Thanks to Joanne, I buckled down and really studied, an activity I didn't have too much experience with in high school.

Once I got home, it was one visit after another. Because my family is so large and because most of them live within a twenty-mile radius of each other, we had many holiday get-togethers and outings. I was enjoying them all with a deep sense of love and belonging . . . this feeling of true connection was still new for me, and I enjoyed it immensely. This was one of the most profound aspects of my last time home, and I'm glad I experienced it.

Another important goal for me was to buy a new computer. This time I was really on my own! The computer I set my sights on was at least fifteen hundred dollars. While I had my big, fancy home-built computer in my dorm room for Xbox games and schoolwork, I didn't have a laptop. My eye was on the new Toshiba that had just come out. It was the king of all laptops at that time. I definitely wanted to take that to classes.

There was no way I was getting one for Christmas. I knew that. I would have to get a winter break job. I needed something that paid enough for me to get that computer in five weeks, the length of our break, and something that offered enough free time for me to feel like I was really on vacation. Mom went to all the big box stores before I came home and had a stack load of applications waiting for me.

I submitted all my applications and got a call from our local Target store for an interview. I flew past the interview process and was then asked to attend an orientation meeting the next day. When I arrived, there were about ten prospective employees waiting in a classroom-like setting. After a short wait, an HR person came in and addressed the group. The first thing she talked about was a "no tolerance" drug policy, and right after that, she asked us to provide a urine test before she continued with the meeting.

At least half of the participants walked out of the room. As one of the few remaining attendees left in the room, I had a private moment of pride and accomplishment that I wasn't one of those who had to make the "walk of shame" out of the Target orientation room. I got a job!

Well, it was everything I wanted. I managed to score about thirty hours a week for the next four weeks. Further, I didn't have to start work until about three p.m., which gave me plenty of time to visit, chill, and enjoy my vacation. If I made it through the next month, I would have enough money to get that computer! Just before I left for school, Dad and I and my winter break savings went laptop shopping, and I came home with my shining trophy. My life was complete!

There was one more wonderful surprise for me this Christmas holiday. Edward came to visit! It was unexpected, and I was so happy to see him. We shared our college experiences, and I pulled Joanne's picture from my wallet and showed it to him. His enthusiastic response, "Yeah, man! She's Filipino! And she's hot!" was music to my ears. It was important to me to have Edward's approval. I told him I was going to marry her.

So far, everything was going splendidly at home. I enjoyed being with my family and getting together with the extended family. I was working toward getting the Toshiba and all was good in the world

... until it wasn't anymore. There were a number of sad and tragic events that put a damper on the otherwise perennially joyous mood of the holiday season.

Heavenly Hindsight

My family visit was wonderfully positive, but as mentioned in the beginning of my story, the universe has a way of making itself known in sometimes harsh ways. All universe events are designed to help us ... believe it or not ... even the sad and tragic ones. If we can just take a peek beyond the veil and understand the true whys of it all, we wouldn't have to feel the pain of loss as much as we do. This particular holiday spoke to the duality of life in the most extreme way.

The Journal

Holiday Tears

A few days after Christmas, Mom got a call from Don, one of her closest friends and my godfather. His wife, Cathy, my sister's godmother, had been killed in a head-on collision with a drunk driver. Cathy was accompanying one of her best friends to the hospital to undergo chemotherapy. Both of them died. Mom was inconsolable.

A couple of days later, my cat, Pouncer, just keeled over and died. He had been sick and was doing better on the prednisone the vet prescribed, but sadly the drug and the disease were just too much for him. He was my buddy and my confidant. I was heartbroken, and my sister was beside herself with shock and grief. Cathy gave Pouncer to Lauren as a birthday gift one year. Lauren never quite got over the fact that Pouncer preferred me over her. All I can say is he was a boy cat and just wanted to be with the guys. It's just odd that they both died in the same week.

I suppose if I thought about what happened over this particular Christmas, I might have thought they were portending something more ominous. I am not a superstitious person, however, so declined going down that road. This might have worked for me except for the chest pains I kept having.

The pains would come and go, but they were kind of intense. I mentioned it to Mom, and she thought I might have indigestion, so she bought me some Tagamet to help my discomfort. I think it helped a little. I still had pain, but it subsided. She also sent me to my doctor, but he really didn't think anything was wrong with me other than a little stress. I didn't bring it up again because I didn't want to upset Mom.

By the third week of January, I was ready to go back to Chico. I was feeling better, I had my new computer, and I had one of the best and saddest Christmas holidays ever. Even so, I was glad to get back to school and Joanne! The events of the holiday, however, left me with an unsettled feeling. I couldn't pinpoint the specific source of the feeling, but it existed nonetheless. I just lived with it for a while.

Back in the Saddle

The second semester was kind of exciting. I had some great classes and had made inroads with the computer department and the professors there. I had my posse of college friends that I tooled around with. I never did get another bike and decided against roller blades, much to Mom's pleasure. So, as most university students, I walked everywhere. If we needed wheels, we had Anthony and his truck. Some of us, names will not be mentioned, had put on a few pounds in the first few months of school and by now were complaining mightily about the excess baggage. We decided to form a bowling team.

It's not like it was a real team. It was a team of "us." We met at the student union for our requisite "workout" time and bowled. What a nerdy, old-fashioned, *wholesome* thing to do . . . and we had the best time ever doing it. I had the perfect platform to tease Chris, Joanne, all of them about their gutter balls. Of course, when it was my turn, I just played it cool. My life had settled into a nice groove.

Aunt Kathy

Around February or so, Mom called to tell me that her aunt Kathy was coming to visit. Kathy was my mom's aunt on her dad's side. At the time, Aunt Kathy was an energetic ball of fire and seventy-eight years old.

After my mom's dad passed, her mother dropped contact with that entire side of the family. It was her uncle Chuck, her dad's younger brother, who found us after a forty-year search. A grand reunion of over one hundred Bartleys was planned for the year 2000 in Las Vegas. My grandfather was an Air Force pilot for one of the first Thunderbird demonstration teams formed in the 1950s. There were at least two other living members of his team that were invited to our reunion. One was an ex-astronaut and another was a current congressman. Not only was the request to hold the reunion event on Nellis Air Force Base accepted, Base Command considered it a VIP event because of the distinguished guests. We also got a free tour of the Thunderbird museum.

Kathy was over the top with joy at our having been found. After the reunion, she came to visit with us each year for about four years, until she had difficulty flying and couldn't come anymore. She would stay anywhere from four to six weeks.

My sister and I loved our aunt Kathy's visits. After the TV show *Jeopardy!* was over, she would pull out her board games and cards, and we would have some special times together. She had a great laugh and was always kidding us. The only time she would get mad was when Mom had to stop our games so we could do homework.

So Kathy was visiting Mom, and she wanted Mom to take her on a road trip to Chico so she could see me and my digs. We set a date for late February of 2003, and Mom, Kathy, and my sister arrived on a Friday afternoon. Mom offered to take me and some of my friends to dinner Saturday night, so I gathered my people together and had them reserve the date. Mom said I could take them anywhere I wanted, so I picked a really nice (expensive) restaurant near downtown. I invited Joanne, my roommate, and a few more friends. We had a great dinner and a great time. Kathy was obviously in heaven, but she, Mom, and Lauren just relaxed that night and let me and my friends take the lead. One of the best dinners ever!

It was on this trip that my mom bought me that dorky Chico State two-piece jumpsuit I mentioned at the beginning of this story. It was the last time I would see them.

In the one or two weeks that followed, I was getting headaches and just didn't feel that well. I had a sense of foreboding or nerves, I don't know what. It was unlike me. To add fuel to the fire, I was under stress because we were thinking about moving out of University Village for our sophomore year and needed to get an apartment. It was a chaotic process. Everybody was thinking the same thing. Every place we looked at had a potential tenant in line in front of us. We needed to find a place, get the application filled out and the money sent in to reserve for the following year. I was getting worried we might not get a place. I had daily phone calls with Mom to get the info I needed to fill out applications. Everything went snail mail in those days, so it took forever. Even though progress was being made, I never did feel quite like myself.

CHAPTER EIGHT

The Truth of Love

Heavenly Hindsight

March 3, 2003

WHEN I LOST CONSCIOUSNESS, I was a little confused but knew with certainty that I had died. As many who have died and come back to tell the tale, I saw the tunnel or something similar and beautiful light beckoning me from the other side. I knew I belonged here and went immediately to the light. Once there, I entered the world of my heaven.

The brightest of white lights penetrated everything. It was so strong and so powerful, yet it didn't burn or hurt. It felt so warm and loving and healing. I was completely absorbed by it. And then I realized I was now part of it. Like a bolt of lightning delivering an unbelievable and ecstatic jolt of love, joy, and bliss, I understood that I was face to face with God.

The love here is so pure, so radiant. I notice that mixed in with the God-love are the loving spirits of all those who lived before as well as the love of those human beings still living on earth. It didn't take long to figure out that anybody or anything that had ever been created in the infinite field has a place right now in this ecstasy.

I understand that I am a critical part of the divine intelligence that exists. I know how I fit in. I know what I have to do. I know the mysteries of the universe. I have met God! I understand how connected each and every living being is . . . and this doesn't just mean humans. It is everything . . . plants, animals, air, water, *everything*. The order is perfect, and how we fit in is perfect for the continuation of this infinite source of love and power.

The seizure I experienced the moment I died was not related to my earthly body, but to my joining of energy with All That Is. It reminded me of a lightning strike. I suffered not one bit when I passed.

The chaos I left behind on earth was expected. The sadness and grief were overwhelming for those I had loved and who had loved me. If they only knew I wasn't gone and the place I've come to is where all will come to as well. This is our home, our true home!

Our life on earth could be compared to being an actor on a stage. We come and go in the guises of different characters and then leave the stage to come home. Each of us has an enormous and important purpose as incarnate beings, but true home is the carrot at the end of the stick.

God is Love . . . That is All

Love. This is one of the easiest things for me to understand. I have known love. I have known my love for others, and I have known others' love for me. Why then is this one of the most difficult states to get to on a consistent basis? I love someone one day and then something happens and I am so upset I can't imagine how I could ever love such a creature. And later, I'm right back to loving them. What's up with this?

I would think that with everything I have read and learned, with all of my loving, emotion-elevating meditations, I would have this down by now. Intellectually, I totally get it. Emotionally, I struggle. This should be the easiest chapter for me to write about, but it's not.

This morning when I got up I reminded myself that writing about love today is on the agenda, and once again, I remembered how difficult this will be. I checked my cellphone for messages and saw that my daughter had sent me the following piece of a meditation that her fiancée had sent to her that day from work.

"Everyone wants to be happy, even those who hurt us. Realizing this helps us create the conditions for understanding and forgiveness."

And then it came to me . . . not that this hasn't been brought up a million times before . . . it just finally *CAME* to me.

I have viewed love as a thing, a form of "tender." I will love those who have earned it, who do the right thing, think and say the right thing. If I'm not pleased, I will show my disappointment by withholding the love until I get what I want. None of this is done with any kind of premeditation. It is simply a habit I have learned over the years that, at times, appeared to be successful. This behavior has been deeply ingrained in my subconscious, where our automatic and autonomous responses reside. I wasn't even aware of this.

But I knew it didn't "feel" right. Something was off. What could I do to understand the feeling of unconditional and true love?

Then I asked, "How am I loving myself?" I really had to think about this. I am very hard on myself. Why? Do I deserve this kind of treatment? No. What is it about me that I can't love unconditionally? Because to be sure, if I can't love myself unconditionally, I won't be able to offer anyone else the same.

In trying to get to the specifics, I came across the following.

"There is no need to ask for love, to need love or crave love, because we are love. You no longer need to pray for wisdom because you are wisdom. You no longer seek peace because your very nature is peace. Standing in that place you have access to all the wisdom, peace, and love in the universe."

—D. Church [1]

The path to true love begins with forgiveness, especially forgiveness of self. Think of it this way. If we truly loved ourselves unconditionally, we could not *possibly* be hurt by others. There really could be nothing that anyone could say or do to us that could hurt us. Rather than that automatic defensive response (withholding love, lashing out, etc.), we would immediately feel compassion for the other. After all, "they just want to be happy" and may be having some trouble finding that happiness.

I needed to forgive myself first. *This* is where the difficulty for me was resting. I could forgive others easier than I could forgive myself. I wasn't looking forward to the work ahead. I really didn't want to pick through all those negative things I had said or done to either myself or others in the past that I might think would be unforgivable. I couldn't imagine anything more depressing.

So I didn't. What I did do was allow myself to "feel" the feeling. In doing so, I bring awareness to the negative emotion I experience. What this does for me is give me an opportunity to evaluate my reaction against the "crime" committed. What I discover is that my responses are generally inappropriate. They don't really match the circumstances of the event. Further, and this is hard to remember, if I find myself judging myself too negatively, I replace that negative thought with a positive one. This has immediate benefits!

What I really uncover, however, is that many of the feelings I harbored, and which are likely responsible for my inappropriate responses, were created eons ago by another experience, probably when I was much younger. Of course, I had forgotten all of this until the day I decided to become aware of it. I suspect, over time, that these original feelings turned into addicting emotions, which I called up because of the false comfort I experienced through them. Yes, these habitual responses originated from a completely different experience but seem to substitute nicely for the situation at hand. What a mess!

This is the place where I begin my work. Becoming aware elevates the problem in such a way that I can really see how I am hurt. Once

I could get back to the source of my pain, it became much easier to forgive myself. Insecurity, lack of self-worth, defensiveness, and a myriad of other negative emotional responses that really started somewhere else and not from the most recent occurrence were at the heart of my problems. In my meditations, I spend a lot of time forgiving myself for not loving myself as well as I could and have had to relearn what was so loving about me in the first place (manifestation). In meditation or prayer or contemplation, you should be able to come up with a pretty long list. It's such an uplifting experience. I discovered I'm not so bad after all!

Once this new feeling is hard-wired, it's hard to go back to being down on yourself. I still have a lot of work to do in this area. Nevertheless, the effect is almost immediate. As I uncovered one reason after another of how lovable I am, I began to change. The cool thing is that I didn't even notice I had changed . . . but a lot of other people did!

I had only been meditating a couple of months when some people at work commented on how "mellow" I was and how I didn't seem to be so uptight. Truly, this was a surprise. I honestly thought the effects would be more subtle. I certainly felt a lot better about myself but didn't expect anyone else to see. I also noticed that more people seemed drawn to me. They were hanging around more. We were having fun.

The fact of the matter is things just do *not* bother me the way they used to. I used to take everything so personally. When I was able to eliminate the reasons for this reaction, it felt like my life just got a little easier. Everything became so much more pleasant. To the givers of my distress, I can see how they just "want to be happy" and can sometimes lash out in frustration. So many times I learned their angst was not even about me, but something else. By removing the obstacles to my own self-love, I was able to make room for others. This was the understanding I craved. Once I had learned to forgive myself, forgiving others was cake-walk.

Now I have a little better acceptance of Dawson Church's belief that we are love, we are wisdom, we are peace. We are getting messages all the time of "you are loved, you are worthy!" Now, I can hear and see them!

> *"We don't see things*
> *As they are;*
> *We see them as we are."*

— **Anais Nin**

Love's Higher View

In the course of my explorations, I stumbled across a little higher view of the idea of authentic, unconditional love . . . the kind of love we need to learn to get anywhere. I remember as a child in religion classes we were taught we are created in the image of God. To be honest, I had a hard time wrapping my head around just this concept. From a child's eyes, I imagined a mirror and instead of seeing myself, I would see God. Many attempts later and I still saw . . . only me. I just figured I didn't know enough to "get it." It wasn't something I spent much time thinking about.

Then I learned something that completely resonated. We are so much more than an image! I come to discover that we, indeed, come from Source, but we started as sparks of light born of the desire of the Divine to express its love in the universe. Mentioned earlier, we aren't just pieces of the Divine, we are fractals of it as we carry the whole of the Divine in our tiny spark of energetic light. You might compare this life to that of a hologram, through which we have the ability to express all kinds of Godly love in a myriad of ways. It is our natural birthright then to be Divine.

> *"You are not a drop in the ocean.*
> *You are the entire ocean in a drop."*

— **Rumi**

This is why so many spiritual journeys encourage us to "go within." The answers are all there. When we can remove the limiting beliefs and the ego constraints that imprison us, we are promised that we can live in the love and light of God. In truth, we would be living in our own light of unconditional love.

Being "In the Flow"

In order to make such dramatic changes in ourselves, we need to be connected to the possibilities and probabilities that are available to us in the divine field. Scientists call this the "non-local" mind. Once we free ourselves of our local minds and move into alignment with the great non-local mind (God), we unlock all the "grace, beauty, synchronicity and wisdom of the universe." [2] We find that we are not alone anymore. We have moved from passenger to driver. We are "in the flow."

The universe, as a loving, intelligent energy as well as the source of all possibility, also has a plan and a "flow." We are either tuned in or we are out of tune. When we are tuned in, we will also be attuned to others who are tuned in. As Dawson Church states, "We *become a beacon of invitation, welcoming those still on the edge to the possibility of joining us.*" People who are experts at being in this state have *very* attractive energies. People are drawn to them. It is a feeling of finally being home, where we all belong.

Why are we so attracted to this essence? Because on some level, we recognize that this essence is who we really are. It *is* us! We have just forgotten. As humans, we must make the choice not only to attune ourselves but continue to choose to attune. The work is never done as long as we exist in the earthly plane. But once we can get ourselves in the flow, it gets easier and easier. You will never want to go back to the old ways again!

Knowledge

We have come to a time in our life on this planet where it is just not enough to know things. We need to know *how* to do things. Knowledge is for the mind. Experience is for the body.

We learn and research and experiment to learn as much as we can about our existence in this life. This is critical and transforming. It is also creative. By learning what we can, we are *adding* new information to the field. What does this mean? How can we add information by studying information that already exists? We exert energy when we learn and we know that energy changes matter. Our point of view, however, is completely unique. No one can see a set of facts in exactly the same way. All of the different iterations of facts are actually new creations of thought that never existed before. We can only learn and see from our own point of view. Spirit does not change from one dimension to another. Only perceptions change, and our points of view are absolutely unique.

Once we are committed to knowledge and learning new things, *then* we can begin to apply that knowledge to changing. There is so much new information out there to learn. I am amazed at the speed with which science has evolved. Very little of what I have discussed in this book was readily available as information forty years ago.

Prejudice against the ideas of the metaphysical was rampant, particularly with respect to how science perceived the field. Further there was a new emergence of Yogis, Gurus, Swamis, Indian mystics and more from parts unknown back in the day. If it weren't for the likes of John Lennon and other celebrities, who traveled far to find their truths, it is unlikely this movement would have spread as quickly as it did.

Getting started on this road is hard. It is hard because we will change! Change is something we have learned to either fear or avoid.

As we know, that's not possible. Change will come to us whether we like it or not or are ready or not. It's much better to be the one in charge of this process than something or someone else.

I have discovered that the more effort and energy I place on this very important job, the less inclination I have to think about all those things I thought I wanted or even needed. Having enough money, having enough things, and having enough time all actually just sort of take care of themselves. That's not to say that I can check out of life and stop doing the work. It just means I don't "think" about having things so much anymore . . . yet they still come. It's a wonderful side benefit. When we become who we truly are, we will be taken care of. This is the gift of abundant synchronicity that our new energy generates.

One Last Thought on Religion

> *If our Religions don't teach us these ideas and don't teach us how connected we are and continue to perpetuate division amongst us, we must find one that does. If we belong to a faith that teaches and practices love for self, love for all and exercises* no judgment, *we will have found a wonderful venue to do our work. What replaces judgment is compassion. What compassion allows is for us to forgive, both ourselves and others. What forgiveness brings is love.*
>
> **—Inspired by J. Van Praagh,**
> **Wisdom From Your Spirit Guides**

No one is punished with eternal damnation or misery. Karma is not for punishment. It is for learning. We were born to heal ourselves, not die. We are getting messages all the time that we are loved enormously. We now know we *are* love, just like our Creator. We will return to love when we have finished our task of healing ourselves completely.

I don't believe we have to give up our faiths to find our purpose, but perhaps we can make mental "adjustments" within ourselves to question that which does not resonate. Pay attention first to your intuition . . . this is your heart speaking. If we neglect our intuition, we are likely to create obstacles and opposition. When we follow the heart, we are "in the flow." Nothing feels forced. When in doubt, find a quiet place and ask your heart what to do.

Wait for what you will learn. You won't be disappointed. Enjoy the journey and don't forget to take in the view! The sights you see will be amazing!

The Journal

Post Mortem

My beautiful Joanne and my roommate, Chris, and friends Anthony and Blake were all in my room when the ambulance took me to the hospital. They followed thinking I had just passed out for a little while and would be just fine.

When they arrived, they were asked to accompany a nurse to a place where she could gently give them the bad news. The nurse then called my parents. At this point, they knew for sure I wasn't coming back. They were given permission to stay with me while they processed their grief. Several hours later, they returned to my dorm to wait for my parents.

Though I was in a new realm, I had to be with everyone in their time of sorrow. Some I visited in dreams, some I left with a warm sense of me. But I was there providing comfort and leaving impressions of the love I felt for all of them.

My mom and dad got the call from the hospital around one a.m. on the morning of March fourth. Within a couple of hours, all of my mom's family came to the house. Mom and Dad were preparing to drive to Chico to collect my things and deal with the business of death: autopsies, funerals, paperwork, and more. Even though my mother objected, my aunt Julie insisted on coming with them. She was right to push. Mom could have handled the ride up to Chico, but not coming back. Dad was in a deep state of shock.

My parents arrived about five a.m. on the morning of March fourth. My posse was there waiting for them. They handled everything with grace, compassion, and a dogged determination not to leave my parents alone. If they only knew how much that really meant to everyone, including myself! By the time they had taken care of all the things people take care of when a loved one dies, it was about three in the afternoon. With the car filled with my belongings and Julie at the wheel, they headed home to our house where the rest of my family was waiting.

The ride home was very quiet. Julie drove, Mom rode shotgun, and Dad sat in the back. I turned my attention to Dad. Of the three of them, Dad was the most in touch with his spirit. He has always had otherworldly gifts such as visions in his head about things he wants to create and dreams for answers to tough questions. As a newbie in the afterlife, I was attracted to his particular energy. I needed to get a message out, and it was through Dad I was able to do that.

As he rested, I spoke to him and wanted him to know how very happy I was. I wanted him to know that I haven't left him at all and will be with him until he joins me. He was in pain, and I needed him to see a different truth about my new existence. I also sent him a very powerful thought that I wanted my ashes scattered from the top of Mt. Linnaeus, that magical mountain we climbed in Utah.

Sometime later, without saying anything to anyone, Dad wrote a poem to put into words what he learned. Dad never considered himself a writer, but this work was the work of angels. I can't tell you how proud I am of the poem he wrote. It captured all I was trying to say to him. In his grief, he heard me.

In June of 2003, Mom and Dad, my sister, Lauren, my uncle Frank, Joanne, Chris, and Anthony made the trip to Utah. Karen from Wilderness Quest met them when they arrived in Moab and drove them to the base of Linnaeus. She gave them instructions on how to hike to the top of the mountain, which would take two or more hours. She waited from a lookout post until they came back, at least five hours later.

I flew the wind that day and connected with loving energies of the canyons and the mountains. It was good.

Virtual Patrick

Patrick! I saw your signal low against the horizon;
like a blinking cursor
In the sky, seeming to say,
"Dad, I'm over here!"
I see you Patrick! Why did you have to go so soon?
We feel so much pain.
I hear your fingers racing across the keyboard to reply,
"It's OK, Dad. I'm doing great!"
Patrick, you're going so fast, I don't get what you mean.
"It's awesome, Dad! I understand the code and it's perfect."
The cursor faded into the dawn's light.
"Patrick, thank you for being my son. I loved you so much."
I see his form facing the light, arms reaching outward, and then
A burst of a billion billion pixels into the Universe.
"Dad, you've got it wrong. I'm not gone.
I've become your Virtual Patrick
And I'm always on for you."

The Afterword

THE MOMENT I LEARNED that our consciousness is immortal, a new world of possibility and potential became available to me. I had always felt immortality to be true, but because there was little proof and so many naysayers, I lingered on the edge of doubt and uncertainty for decades. For some reason, it is important to me that I continue to live after I leave this dimension of life. It is really hard for me to imagine, having already suffered so much, that physical death could be the absolute end to our troubles. What a waste that would be!

To the contrary, everything that we learn, every experience we have while we are here living on earth, every thought, every creative idea, just about everything we have or have done we take with us when we move on. We will either grow in love and compassion and service to others while we are here or we will be preparing a knapsack of lessons to take into our next life, which will feel a lot heavier than when we left, by the way. Either way, we bring everything with us.

Since we know we are immortal, we have some basic responsibilities while we are here in this time and place. Though we are charged with learning lessons in each life that will help us move closer to Source, we do have the gift of free will and, therefore, can decide not to do anything. No harm, no foul, but all karmic debts must eventually be cleared.

Throughout the writing of this book, I keep thinking about how I felt just before I put pen to paper. I have a wonderful home, husband, good friends, community, hobbies, and work, yet throughout it all, I remained unhappy. Unable to pinpoint anything in my environment that was out of kilter, I could only determine that my state of unhappiness lived inside of me and I had no idea what the problem or problems were. It was this agitation, this feeling that led me to knowledge. Reading proved to be the first remedy as the more I learned, the better I started to feel. It was also a new feeling of "resonation" that inspired me to continue on. When I came across a new piece of information or a new concept, I often felt completely harmonious with the information I was learning. I felt truth at the core. I had no doubts, no real questions, just a "knowing" that this is true for me. It was the reading that I did that presented the first and one of the most important catalysts for my transformation.

> *"Your responsibility to God is to discover, to accept, and to express this greater purpose that has brought you into the world. To do this you must follow knowledge allowing knowledge to be mysterious, for it exists beyond the realm of your intellect."*
>
> **—The New Message from God, www.newmessage.org**

So, while we might not use a soul journey to ascend, we are responsible for acquiring knowledge and, hopefully, wisdom. Since we are charged with expressing who we are through a physical body, what we learn and how we use this knowledge determines the quality and power of that which we create. What and how we choose to learn then becomes very important.

For me, it all started with questions . . . and a *lot* of them. I have since discovered that starting one's pilgrimage with questions is very effective. The desire to have them addressed led me to reading material that just happened to have the right answers! While I believe my intuition led the way, and it did, it was the questions I asked that served as the scouting party and were sent ahead to find the path.

> *"Part of our journey is to return to the power and presence of knowledge. Here we do not live according to answers, but you live with questions. You live with questions you may never be able to answer, but you live with them because they open your mind and they stimulate a deeper connection with knowledge and yourself."*
>
> **—Revealed to Marshall Vian Summers, 10/08/08,**
> **www.newmessage.org**

I did not know I was responsible for so much in this lifetime. It's been hard enough as it is just to navigate the illusions and emotions and this veil of forgetfulness that plagues us. That has kept me busy for a long time! Now, I know the real purpose, the real mission and point of our being here . . . we need to learn and grow and create so that we can heal! We are preparing ourselves for glory and have a lot of work to do. We will all get there! Rest assured. But how fast and when? The better question would be how are we doing it?

A soul journey is certainly one way, but there are others. Some may be so advanced on their path on earth that they arrive with more of those qualities that will point to a successful incarnation . . . an open heart is one example.

> *"Fortunately, some are born with spiritual immune systems that, sooner or later, give rejection to the illusory worldview grafted upon them from birth through social conditioning. They begin sensing that something is amiss and start looking for answers. Inner knowledge and anomalous outer experiences show them a side of reality others are oblivious to, and so begins their journey of awakening. Each stop of the*

journey is made by following the heart instead of following the crowd and by choosing knowledge over the veils of ignorance."

—Henri Bergson

As mightily as I fought this path over the years, I found myself drawn to the very thing I avoided and what would eventually heal me. My questions regarding my son's death were answered, and I have so much comfort from that as a result. What I didn't know is that I would have a legion of spiritual helpers to assist me. I certainly didn't have a plan, but that is the beauty of knowledge. As we learn, we attract like energy to bolster the quest.

This is the thing about soul journeys. You get your answers, job, house, husband, and money, etc. But it doesn't end there. Doors are constantly being opened. There is so much more to explore! I've discovered this and also relished in the benefits that have come my way. All that was required of me was to make the commitment to learn. The rest seems to be taking care of itself quite nicely.

Acknowledgments

IT'S A SHAME THAT Acknowledgments are placed at the end of a book . . . like some sort of afterthought. Know from this Author that if I could have reasonably presented neon lights and a brass band to thank you, I would have. It is the quiet support over months and months and sometimes, years, that means so much. The quiet celebrators are a hardy lot. They just keep on truckin'!

Early Beta Readers: Velma Cleasby, Candy Hill, Elaine Pasquini, and Rev. Dr. Barbara Meyers. Many, many thanks for slogging through those rough, early pages. All your comments were taken to heart and resulted in many substantive changes.

Editing: To my first editor, Katherine Sands, who saw something in my writing. Thank you for taking on my project.

Most Supportive Fans: To Elaine Pasquini and Odette Fournier, thank you for always asking; thank you for giving me the reasons to continue. And to Nancy Gallenson, for helping me to share my story.

Family: To my husband, Alan, and daughter, Lauren Aughney . . . for being all of the above, thank you! And in the most elevated position is my son, Patrick, for his special assistance to this incarnate being and for his inspiration to her effort. There is no doubt about it . . . you have proven you are here with us all.

Notes

Chapter Two: The Subject of Truths

[1]   Schwartz, R. *Your Soul's Plan: Discovering the Real Meaning of the Life You Planned Before You Were Born.* Frog Books, Berkeley, 2007, 2009.

[2]   Cannon, D. *The Convoluted Universe: Book One.* Ozark Mountain Press, 2001, 2007.

[3]   Dispenza, J. *Becoming Supernatural: How Common People are Doing the Uncommon.* Hay House, 2012.

[4]   Cannon, D. *The Convoluted Universe: Book One.* Ozark Mountain Press, 2001, 2007.

[5]   Dispenza, J. *Evolve Your Brain: The Science of Changing Your Mind.* Health Communications, Inc., 2007.

[6]   Feick, M. *A Radical Approach to the Akashic Records: Master Your Life and Raise Your Vibration.* M. Feick, 2018.

[7]   Dispenza, J. *Evolve Your Brain.* Hay House, 2007. p65.

[8]   Newton, M. *Life-Between-Lives: Stories of Personal Transformation.*

[9]   Newton, M. *Memories of the Afterlife.*

Chapter Three: The Truth of Lessons

[1] Weiss, B. *Many Lives, Many Masters.* Simon & Shuster, 1988.

[2] Cannon, D. *The Convoluted Universe: Book One.* Ozark Mountain Publishing, 2001, 2007.

[3] Weiss, B. *Many Lives, Many Masters.* Touchtone.

[4] Braden, G. *Using the Heart-Brain to Face Everyday Challenges.* YouTube, 9/18/2018.

[5] Braden, G. *Human by Design: From Evolution By Chance to Transformation by Choice.* Hay House, 2017.

Chapter Four: The Truth of Energy

[1] purelysimpleorganicliving.com.

[2] Dispenza, J. *Evolve Your Brain: The Science of Changing Your Mind.* Health Communications, Inc., 2007.

[3] Dispenza, J. *Breaking the Habit of Being Yourself: How to Lose Your Mind and Create a New One.* Hay House, 2012.

[4] Hicks, E&J. *The Law of Attraction: The Basics of the Teachings of Abraham.* Hay House, 2006.

[5] Dispenza, J. *Becoming Supernatural.* Hay House, 2017.

[6] Church, D. *Mind to Matter.* Hay House, 2018.

[7] Dispenza, J. *You Are the Placebo.* Hay House, 2014.

[8] Watkins, S. *Conversations with Seth, Book 2, 25th Anniversary Ed.* Moment Point Press, 1980, 2006.

[9]   Dispenza, J. *Becoming Supernatural: How Common People are Doing the Uncommon.* Hay House, 2017.

[10]   Dispenza, J. *You Are the Placebo: Making Your Mind Matter.* Hay House, 2014.

[11]   whatisepigenetics.com

[12]   www.science.org.au.

[13]   Abstract. www.ncbi.nim.nih.gov.

[14]   Dispenza, J. *You Are the Placebo*, Hay House, 2014.

[15]   Cannon, D. *The Convoluted Universe: Book One.* Ozark Mountain Publishing, 2001, 2007.

[16]   Dispenza, J. *Breaking the Habit of Being Yourself: How to Lose Your Mind and Create a New One.* Hay House, 2012.

[17]   Cannon, D. *The Convoluted Universe: Book Three.* Ozark Mountain Publishing, 2008.

[18]   Weiss, B. *Many Lives, Many Masters.* Hay House, 1988.

[19]   Newton, M. *Journey of Souls.* Llewellyn, 1994, 2003.

Chapter Five: The Truth of Creation

[1]   Church, D. *Mind to Matter.* Hay House, 2018.

[2]   Church, D. *Mind to Matter.* p33.

[3]   Cannon, D. *The Convoluted Universe: Book Three.*

[4]   Church, D. *Mind to Matter*, 2018.

[5]   Church, D. *Mind to Matter*, 2018. p. 262.

[6]   Yates, J. *The Mind Illuminated: A Complete Meditation Guide Integrating Buddhist Wisdom and Brain Science for Greater Mindfulness*. Atria Paperback, Simon & Schuster, 2015, 2019.

[7]   Dass, R. *Be Here Now*. Harper Collins, 2010.

Chapter Six: The Truth of Free Will

[1]   Dispenza, J. *Becoming Supernatural*. Hay House, 2017.

[2]   Church, D. *Mind to Matter*. Hay House, 2018.

[3]   Stoller, G. *My Life After Life: A Posthumous Memoir*. Dream Treader Press, Santa Fe, 2011.

[4]   Frankl, V. *Man's Search for Meaning*. Beacon Press, 1959, 2006.

[5]   Stoller, G. *My Life After Life*. Dream Treader.

[6]   Church, D. *Mind to Matter*. Hay House, 2018.

Chapter Seven: The Truth of Connection

[1]   Church, D. *Mind to Matter*. Hay House, 2018, p.96.

[2]   Weiss, B. *Miracles Happen: The Transformational Healing Power of Past-Life Memories*. Harper One, 2012.

[3]   Weiss, B. *Many Lives, Many Masters*. Touchstone (S&S), 1988. p. 35.

[4]   Cannon, D. *The Three Waves of Volunteers and the New Earth*, 2011.

[5]   Sanderson, C. *The Reluctant Messenger: An Ordinary Person's Extraordinary Journey Into the Unknown.* Clark Press, 2018.

[6]   Sanderson, C. *The Reluctant Messenger Returns: An Unexpected Adventure Into the Angelic Realms.* Clark Press, 2020.

Chapter Eight: The Truth of Love

[1]   Church, D. *Mind to Matter.* Hay House, 2018, p.277.

[2]   Church, D. *Mind to Matter.* Hay House, 2018, p.277.

Bibliography

Science, Energy, Healing, Manifestation: The Power Humans Have to Change Thoughts Into Matter

Dispenza, J. *Evolve Your Brain: The Science of Changing Your Mind.* Health Communications, Inc., 2007.

—. *Breaking the Habit of Being Yourself: How to Lose Your Mind and Create a New One.* Hay House, 2012.

—. *You Are the Placebo: Making Your Mind Matter.* Hay House, 2014.

—. *Becoming Supernatural: How Common People are Doing the Uncommon.* Hay House, 2017.

Church, D. *Mind to Matter: The Astonishing Science of How Your Brain Creates Material Reality.* Hay House, 2018.

Braden, G. *Human by Design: From Evolution By Chance to Transformation By Choice.* Hay House, 2017.

Hicks, E&J. *The Law of Attraction: The Basics of the Teaching of Abraham.* Hay House, 2006.

Past-Life Regressions, Life-Between-Lives, Planning Our Incarnations

Weiss, B. *Many Lives, Many Masters: The True Story of a Prominent Psychiatrist, His Young Patient, and the Past Life Therapy that Changed Both Their Lives.* Touchstone, Simon & Schuster, 1988.

—. *Through Time Into Healing: Discovering the Power of Regression Therapy to Erase Trauma and Transform Mind, Body, and Relationships.* Touchtone, 1992, 1993.

—. *Same Soul, Many Bodies: Discover the Healing Power of Future Lives Through Progression Therapy.* Free Press, Simon & Schuster, 2004.

—. *Miracles Happen: The Transformational Healing Power of Past Life Memories.* Harper One, 2012.

Newton, M. *Journey of Souls: Case Studies of Life Between Lives.* Llewellyn Publishing, 1994, 2003.

—. *Life Between Lives: Hypnotherapy for Spiritual Regression.* Llewellyn Publishing, 2004, 2013.

—. *Memories of the Afterlife: Life-Between-Lives Stories of Personal Transformation.* Llewellyn Publishing, 2009, 2010.

Schwartz, R. *Your Soul's Plan: Discovering the Real Meaning of the Life You Planned Before You Were Born.* Frog Books, Berkeley, 2007, 2009.

—. *Your Soul's Gift: The Healing Power of the Life You Planned Before You Were Born.* R. Schwartz, 2012.

Kelley, M. *Beyond Past Lives: What Parallel Realities Can Teach Us About Relationships, Healing and Transformation.* Hay House, 2014.

Elsen, P. *When Souls Awaken: Real Life Accounts from Past Life-Between-Lives Regression.* Pieter Elsen, 2019.

Kagan, A. *The Afterlife of Billy Fingers: How My Bad-Boy Brother Proved to Me There is Life After Death.* Hampton Roads Publishing, 2013.

Byrd, C. *The Boy Who Knew Too Much: An Astounding True Story of a Young Boy's Past Life Memories.* Hay House, 2017.

Stoller, G. *My Life After Life: A Posthumous Memoir.* Dream Treader Press, Santa Fe, 2011.

The Mysteries of the Universe, the Shift, Moving From 3D to 5D

Cannon, D. *The Convoluted Universe: Book One.* Ozark Mountain Publishing, 2001, 2007.

—. *The Convoluted Universe: Book Two.* Ozark Mountain Publishing, 2011.

—. *The Convoluted Universe: Book Three.* Ozark Mountain Publishing, 2008.

—. *The Three Waves of Volunteers and the New Earth.* Ozark Mountain Publishing, 2011.

Sanderson, C. *The Reluctant Messenger: An Ordinary Person's Extraordinary Journey Into the Unknown.* Clark Press, 2018.

—. *The Reluctant Messenger Returns: An Unexpected Adventure Into the Angelic Realms.* Clark Press, 2020.

St. Germaine, M. *Waking Up in 3D: A Practical Approach to Multidimensional Transformation.* Bear & Company.

Carwin, J. *Pleidian Prophecy 2020: The New Golden Age.* J Carwin.

The Answers are "Inside," Meditating in the NOW Moment

Tolle, E. *The Power of Now: A Guide to Spiritual Enlightenment*. New World Library and Namaste Printing, 1999, 2004.

Dass, R. *Be Here Now*. Enhanced Edition. Harper Collins E-Books, 2010.

—. *Be Love Now: The Path of the Heart*. Harper Collins E-Books, 2010.

Yates, J. *The Mind Illuminated: A Complete Meditation Guide Integrating Buddhist Wisdom and Brain Science for Greater Mindfulness*. Atria Paperback, 2015, 2019.

Miscellaneous Support and Inspiration

Van Praagh, J. *Wisdom From Your Spirit Guides: A Handbook to Contact Your Soul's Greatest Teachers*. Hay House, 2017.

Bernstein, G. *Spirit Junkie: A Radical Road to Self-Love and Miracles*. Harmony Books, 2011.

Watkins, S. *Conversations With Seth, Book 2: 25th Anniversary Edition*. Moment Point Press, 1981, 1999, 2006.

Ruiz, D.M. *The Four Agreements: A Practical Guide to Personal Freedom*. A Toltec Wisdom Book. Amber-Allen Publishing, 1997.

Feick, M. *A Radical Approach to the Akashic Records: Master Your Life and Raise Your Vibration*. M. Feick, 2018.

Redfield, J. *The Celestine Prophecy: An Adventure*. Grand Central Publishing, 1993, 2006.

Frankl, V. *Man's Search for Meaning*. Beacon Press, 1959, 2006.

CPSIA information can be obtained
at www.ICGtesting.com
Printed in the USA
LVHW092142171221
706497LV00001B/16